Jo Foley

Great Spa Escapes

Elegant

Exotic

Opulent

Serene

Spiritual

Sensuous

Spa is an international word – one whose meaning is the same in any language. What began as a place name in small town Belgium, spread throughout Europe as a generic for any place where mineral springs or healing waters popped out of the ground to lavish their therapeutic properties on the ill, the over-indulgent or the mildly dyspeptic. Over the last two centuries it spread out across the world to mean a place where people go to rest and repair. A centre where waters could be taken, or where one could bathe in their curative properties. Gradually other treatments were offered to visitors – chiropody, osteopathy, physiotherapy, nutritional guidance – mostly with a medical or pseudo-medical background, these were places, after all, for the afflicted. Diets were prescribed while fresh air and rest were paramount to ensure the visitor left looking and feeling better.

And while a few such places still exist today (they can be found mostly in central Europe), a different kind of spa can be experienced wherever else you go in the world. The premise is still the same – to help people look and feel better – but they are light years away from their eighteenth century forebears. Instead the spa perpetrators went further back in time to the opulence and luxury of the Roman baths with their marble and mosaics, to the hammams of the Ottoman empire with their steams, heat and scents, and to the traditions of some of the oldest medical disciplines on earth – China and to India, while en route they discovered the traditions and therapies of Indonesia, Malaysia and the temples of Thailand. For not only is spa an international word, it is these days, a truly international experience.

From downtown Miami to the great spaces of southern Africa, from tiny atolls in the Maldives to the foothills of the Himalayas and from the jungles of northern Thailand to the middle of the Pacific Ocean there is a spa waiting to envelop, pamper and caress the careworn, the stressed and the seriously tired. Each more luxurious than the last, each offering a panoply of treatments which have been plundered from across the globe. You can get a lomi lomi massage thousands of miles from its native Polynesia, acupuncture and tui'na from Chinese medicine can be enjoyed from Africa to Italy, while shiatsu from Japan, shirodara from India and lulur from Java can be found in any spa worth the name between Florida and France. And it continues with new therapies deriving from the ancient lore of the aboriginals, the plants and stones from Native Americans, and the traditions of Indonesian royals as well as state of the art treatments from the laboratories of the major American and European beauty houses.

Into this great melting pot of spa ingredients come the practitioners – the masseurs, the facialists, the manicurists, the crystal healers, the doctors and the chiropractors, the yoga gurus and the dance masters, the life coaches and the acupuncturists – all, every single one of these people, these traditions, ingredients and therapies, geared to helping some of the most over-indulged people ever, to feel better about themselves, about their bodies and about their lives. For this more than anything accounts for the great growth of spas – the real need people have to escape the strains of modern life to chill-out and relax.

In an over-stretched, over-stressed world the greatest luxury of all is time. Time for yourself. Choosing an island, an hotel, an escape with a spa is literally giving yourself permission to use that time. Spas provide refuge and offer repair.

In a world where more and more people live alone either through choice or circumstance, spas provide a safe haven where they can relax and not feel out of place, where they can surrender to the healing power of touch. People who live alone do not have the same opportunities of touch as those who live with partners and families – witness how the elderly who are on their own constantly stroke their hands or arms, remember that new born babies can die if they are not held or touched. Touch is powerful, it soothes, heals and comforts. A pedicure can put a smile on someone's face not just because the callouses have been removed, but because that person has been massaged and touched. The divorced and the widowed, the vulnerable and the lonely can find solace in a place which is devoted to serenity and wellbeing, and this helps the healing process.

But most important, spas are fun – they are also legal, sexy and don't make you fat. They are a sybarite's paradise. The thought, time and money spent on them is nothing if not lavish – silk walls, satin cushions, soft lights, scented candles, incense, cashmere wraps, slippers, sarongs, organic foods and juices. How can anyone not feel better under such a plethora of pleasure inducers. (If only they could learn to can the music – unless of course the guest has a penchant for panpipes, humpback whales or seagulls. Silence, they might well remember, is the best sound of all). Spas are often in the forefront of hotel excellence in design and service and mostly they are situated in some of the most beautiful places on earth. They pamper and spoil, they soothe and smooth – they indulge our every whim.

Elegant
Graceful
Correct
Chic
Stylish
Refined

Elegance is calm, controlled and appropriate. It is confident and understated. An elegant spa is one that is refined in its philosophy, knows what it is about and what it offers. It is pleasing to the eye. Elegance has little to do with fashion or fads – it is more a sense of itself. It is relentless in its pursuit of perfection, in its search for the acceptable shade of parchment, the palest granite or the rose petal picked at dawn – yet it always appears effortless. There is ease about elegance, and yet it is the result of a rigorous aesthetic.

Elegance is always appropriate to its place, its time and its purpose. In an elegant spa everything is the result of careful choosing – from the therapies on offer to the robes, the oils, the music and the décor, nothing jars. In an elegant spa nothing is left to chance – therapies, lotions, specialists are all part and parcel of a very assured sense of itself. Elegance is nothing, if not about comfort, making the guest feel reassured and welcome, producing the most pleasing environment and offering the most desirable treatments. Who could want for more?

The Better Living Institute, Hotel Royal, Evian-Les-Bains, France.

Evian-Les-Bains

I f water is the source of life, then Evian, surely, must be the place
to find it. With the snow-covered Alps, whose glittering peaks are
home to glaciers, waterfalls and streams, in the background, and
Lake Geneva, the largest and one of the clearest lakes in Europe,
closer to hand, Evian-Les-Bains lives up to its name and reputation.

Since 1789, when the virtues of the waters were first discovered,
the town has attracted visitors from all over Europe, reaching the
pinnacle of its fame in the early years of the last century, when it
was heralded as the grandest of all the Belle Époque spa towns.
It was for this reason that the Hotel Royal was built – to provide a
home away from home where the crowned heads of Europe could
frolic and play while pursuing a healthy regime. The grandeur of
its architecture and the opulence of its furnishings, not to mention
the sweep of parkland fronting the lake, made it a place fit for a
king (which must be why Edward VII was asked to be the first guest
at the hotel in 1909).

There are three spas in Evian-les-Bains, each of which fulfils
a separate function. The Better Living Institute, based in the Hotel
Royal itself, has a range of custom-made health, beauty and fitness
programmes. It's not a place of self-denial, though, as the regime
includes some of the most delectable food you are ever likely to
eat. The Espace Forme, the spa at the Hotel Ermitage, focuses
on baths and beauty treatments, and boasts a gym and a pool
to boot. The Thermes Evian, which is based in town, is a huge
hydrotherapy centre, with massages, showers, blitzes and baths
designed to soothe every type of ache and comfort those seeking
complete relaxation.

The Better Living Institute prides itself, in particular, on its special
three-to seven-day programmes. One of the most popular is known
as the Re-Energy programme – a combination of relaxation and
underwater massage on alternate days, plus aquagym and a choice
of algae wraps and baths which will help boost circulation, improve
muscle tone and smooth the skin.

A special weekend programme can include features of body
remodelling or any one of the other programmes. There's the
Lightness Programme, for instance, which includes everything
from facials to oriental velvet body peeling, Mass Active slimming
treatment, cellulite massage and foot reflexology, a special slimming

A balance of clear, clean fresh air, deep
breathing and gentle exercise brings
about a strong sense of well-being.

programme designed for men or the extraordinarily popular mother and baby programme at the Thermes Evian. Here, both mother and baby have daily massages and swimming sessions, followed by mum getting on with the hard work of regaining her figure and energy levels through a combination of exercise, diet and massage.

Each element of the programmes can be booked individually, whether you're after a facial with a heated face mask, formulated to restore contours you thought had been lost forever; a reiki treatment; aromatherapy or shiatsu massages or a number of mud and algae wraps. One of the most relaxing therapies, ideal after a long journey, is a spell in the Relaxman, a flotation capsule. You lie in the enclosed, warm, liquid darkness, suspended in time and space, for three-quarters of an hour. It's a bit like being back in the womb, but I wouldn't recommend it if you're at all claustrophobic.

Of course the one thing you must do at Evian is indulge in a water treatment – there are any number to choose from on the menu. When in relaxing mode, try balneotherapy – a warm bath in which 180 water jets are let loose on every part of your body, from the soles of your feet to the nape of your neck, massaging, pulverising, stimulating and, finally, relaxing. Although the massage is very gentle, the frequency of those jets hitting you has a cumulative effect that is immensely strong – when you eventually emerge from this bath of pleasure, you really have no choice but to rest for a quarter of an hour. After that, you will feel so energised that you can either spend the rest of the day enthusiastically hiking around the lake or the woods behind it, or spend the night (quite literally) at the casino in town.

The Sanctuary, The Residence, Mauritius.

The Sanctuary

Mauritius is truly in the middle of nowhere. Actually, to be more accurate, it's more than a thousand miles from the east coast of Africa on one side and the southwest coast of India on the other. Its strategic position was bitterly fought over for many years by traders from Holland, France and Britain who, over time, endowed the islands with a multi-cultural heritage that has only been enhanced by the more recent arrival of immigrants from India, Africa and the Far East. In the towns, Hindu temples rub shoulders with Buddhist centres, Christian churches, Chinese shops, East African market squares and government offices built by the French. No longer the centre of mid-ocean conflict, the island is now best known for the friendliness of its people, its sugar production, the extinct dodo and some of the most luxurious hotels in the world. One of these is The Residence.

From the minute you step through its front door, you enter not just a different world but also a different era, as the vast, soaring, airiness of this hotel harks back to the days of Mauritius's great plantation houses. With its lofty, fan-swept ceilings and colonial style rattan furniture, the reception area sets the scene. From here it's just a few steps to The Veranda, which opens out on to the garden, the swimming pool and the beach, which is accessed by great curving stairs. The atmosphere evoked is one of space, light and unhurried grace.

The aura of luxurious elegance is carried over into the services offered by the hotel. A helicopter pad on the beach makes for a truly memorable arrival, a butler is assigned to each room, three restaurants offer everything from local specialities to gourmet experiences and The Bar, which runs almost half the length of the hotel, could have come straight from a Somerset Maugham novel.

The Residence is permeated by a distinctive fragrance – the unmistakable scent of ylang-ylang. The plant was only introduced to Mauritius (probably from Indonesia) during the 18th century by Pierre Poivre, a merchant, and now flourishes almost everywhere on the island. Dubbed the flower of flowers by parfumiers, ylang-ylang's essential oil is used as the base note in many perfumes. The Residence has taken the flower to its heart: in season there are great bowls of it everywhere, and every evening a few drops

of the oil are placed on ceramic rings heated by the warmth of the bedside lamps so that every room is scented. Unsurprisingly, ylang-ylang is used extensively in the potions and lotions available at the hotel's spa, The Sanctuary.

The Sanctuary has its own menu of aromatic baths and wraps, as well as bust-toning and lymphatic drainage treatments, but it is the La Prairie treatments, based around the philosophy of the Swiss company, that make the spa stand out. So stringent are La Prairie's requirements for spas wishing to use its products that there are only a handful of places throughout the world that qualify. Both men and women can benefit from a number of special facials and body treatments designed to promote cellular regeneration. There's one for balancing dry and oily skins, another for detoxing the tired, while untoned, very sensitive skins will benefit from a special desensitising treatment and, of course, there's La Prairie's world-renowned age-management treatments for over-exposed and mature skins.

Finally, there's the most famous and luxurious treatment of all: the caviar face and body treatment, which is based on the essence contained in the tiny eggs. La Prairie has managed to stabilise the enzymes, minerals and essences contained in sturgeon's roe and transform them into creams, masques, potions and lotions, and these are used at the Sanctuary to cleanse, buff, massage and rehydrate both face and body. My Sanctuary favourite is the La Prairie special. It involves the caviar, of course, but is actually focused around a cellular lipo-sculpting treatment. I like it because, not only do I get massaged with a deliciously rich cream, I can also kid myself that I'll be a little leaner and tauter afterwards. Whether that's all in my mind or not is a moot point, but the treatment makes me feel fantastic – and my skin glows like silk afterwards.

Il Centro Benessere, Palazzo della Fonte, Fiuggi, Italy.

Palazzo della Fonte

They say that Michelangelo came to Fiuggi to take the waters. Without a doubt, many popes, both before and after him, visited the little town and its beneficial springs. They came to find relief for digestive problems and respite from gout, for the thermal waters of this town, which nestles in the Ernici mountain range, almost midway between Naples and Rome. Visitors still flock – these days in their thousands – to the vast mushroom-shaped complex of the public spa at Fonte Bonifacio in search of the curative waters. This main spring is situated amid formal gardens in the lower, newer, part of town, which is also where you'll find most of the shops, cafés and traffic. High above, looking down upon the modern centre from the mountain heights, is the older, prettier Fiuggi Alta, an old town of narrow streets, ancient walls, charming piazzas and historic church. Between the two, in the centre of an elegant park surrounded by woodlands of chestnuts and pine, stands a huge, impressive Art Nouveau structure – the Grand Hotel Palazzo della Fonte – which has its own impressive history. It opened in 1913, and has since provided kings, presidents, consuls and ambassadors with a home from home while they enjoyed the waters, with a brief lull during the Second World War, when it became first a Red Cross centre and then the Allied Forces' headquarters.

Some 12 years ago, the hotel was restored to its former glory, and is now one of the most luxurious pleasure palaces in Italy. With its elegant terraces, grand dining rooms and awe-inspiring lobby, you can see what pulled in the aristocracy, but now you can also benefit from the recent addition of a glamorous spa. Il Centro Benessere is on the lower floor of the hotel, and many of its rooms look out either onto the gardens or the underlit indoor pool, whose surrounds open out onto a large sunny terrace. There are saunas, a steam room, hydrotherapy units, consultation rooms, the ultimate in gyms and a large beauty area – to Italians, health and beauty are near indivisible. The holistic approach to well-being, which acknowledges that balance of mind, spirit, body and emotions is vital, that pervades the spa stems from the old Roman belief in mens sana in corpore sano – a healthy mind in a healthy body.

There are more than 40 treatments on the spa menu to help you achieve both, as well as a number of packages and programmes.

Water is the essence of Fiuggi from the thermal waters, which first brought visitors to the glamour of the Palazzo's indoor swimming pool.

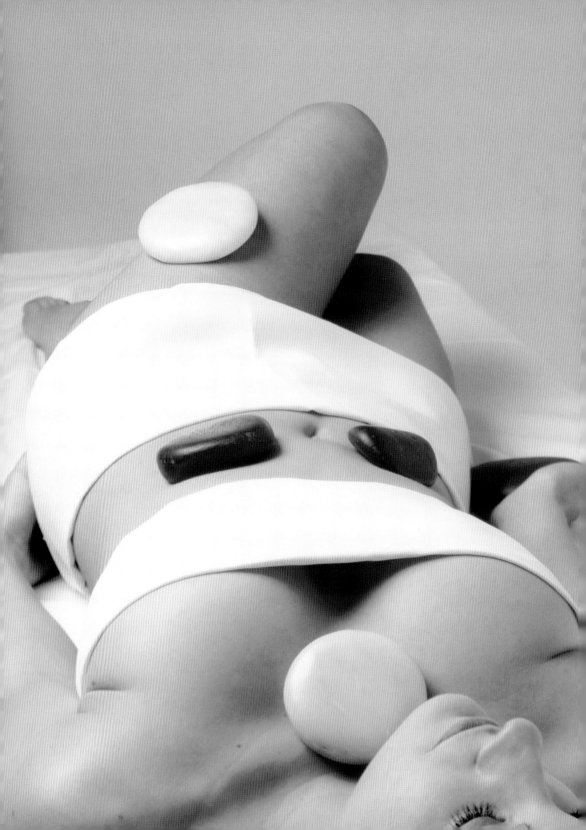

Thanks to its watery heritage, a number of treatments involve hydrotherapy, to which end there are special baths, massage tubs and jet sprays. The designated beauty area has a plethora of skincare treats to choose from. These include a face-lifting therapy in which low-voltage electrical charges stimulate the skin cells as well as the underlying muscles to promote new growth in one and help lift the other. The effect – and it helps if you have a minimum of three treatments – is to make the baggy bits under the eyes and around the jowls sit up rather than sag, and plump out the skin, softening the look of any lines or wrinkles. It's easy to become addicted to the treatments as you begin to notice a difference very soon after the first few.

In between, there are all kinds of massage, from the underwater variety to aromatherapy and lymphatic, shiatsu and hot stone. There are also almost a dozen different facials, plus a whole range of peels. Injections of collagen are also available, and these are used to 'fill' fine lines and wrinkles. Fiuggi also offers a number of specialist therapies. These include rebirthing – a serious method of deep breathing based heavily on yogic practice teamed with guided meditation. The idea is to clear the mind of clutter and irrelevance, in order to create a regenerating effect. Rebirthing is particularly good for the over-stressed and over-worked, but it places heavy demands on the participant, who needs to find a reserve of inner strength and willpower to achieve the desired results. Clearing a full and busy mind takes time and effort.

Nutrition has an important part to play in the spa's holistic philosophy, and a consultation with the resident nutritionist can help with weight loss, get rid of food allergies or simply produce a healthy eating plan. Its six-day slimming package is highly sought-after, and includes a medical check, a nutrition lesson, a tailor-made diet, five body treatments, six water gym classes, four saunas and steams, five muscle-toning treatments, three facial treatments and two colon cleansings specials. Although the regime is disciplined, rest assured that, thanks to the culinary passion of the Italians, the food, although low in calories, will be delicious. So give Fiuggi a few days of your time – you may well end up feeling as if you've undergone a Renaissance of your very own.

Clinique La Prairie

The shores of Lake Geneva, just a few kilometres from Montreux, are home to one of the most extraordinary health resorts in the world. Almost concealed from prying eyes by woodland stands La Prairie – part clinic, part hospital, part research centre and quite possibly the most serious spa in the world.

The Clinique La Prairie is not your average spa, of course. Founded in 1931, it is best known for its revitalisation centre, where a cellular rejuvenation treatment, based on extracts derived from foetal sheep cells, is used to build up the body's immune system. This exclusive treatment was developed by the clinic's founder, Professor Paul Niehans, the illegitimate son of the last Kaiser, who, during his lifetime treated popes and princes as well as stars of screen and sport. Several decades on, celebrities still mingle with captains of industry and great beauties in their pursuit of eternal youth.

The somewhat anonymous glass-fronted building where these miracles take place is set back a little from the road. Only when you walk through to the gardens do you see the elegant old villa where the dream of finding a path to rejuvenation was born. It has now become an administrative centre, with most guests being housed in the modern structure.

Treatments at the clinic are taken very seriously – they begin with a full medical examination that includes blood tests and X-rays, with further tests to ascertain that your body will not reject the live extracts. The therapy itself involves two injections over a period of two days. As the injections are intramuscular, they are given slowly, each taking about five minutes per buttock. But, although you can feel the needle going in, there is no pain. If you are squeamish like me, you can pretend that nothing is happening and have a conversation with the nurse about what she did on her holidays. When it's all over, you rest for half an hour, after which you can get up and go swimming, have a facial or go for a walk. I must admit that after the last injection I decided I wanted to see the needle. I'm glad I left it until the end… It was one of the longest I've ever seen. In addition to its longed-for anti-ageing properties, recent research suggests that the treatments can help delay the onset of degenerative diseases

such as arthritis, as well as making chemotherapy and radiation therapy more tolerable.

Most visitors opt to combine the treatment with the Beauty Med, a six-part daily treatment which teams highly sophisticated equipment with the latest developments in skin care. First comes the Corpotrim, a machine developed by NASA scientists, in which electrodes are strapped to your stomach and thighs. These cause your muscles to contract and the frequency is gradually increased – a 17-minute session is said to be the equivalent of an hour of aerobics. While the lower half of your body is contracting like mad, another machine, the Corpolux, is used on the upper half. This uses light, which is absorbed by the skin's pigment, where it is transformed into chemical energy which treats a range of complaints, from acne and wrinkles to stress. A further machine, the Corpomed, has more electrodes, which are attached to feet, hands, chest, arms and knees to help eliminate toxins via the lymphatic system. The Corpofit tightens flabby facial muscles, while the Corpodem uses lasers to stimulate cell renewal and soften wrinkles. Even if you're one of the unlucky few whose system rejects the cell therapy, a Beauty Med programme not only makes you feel better, it sure helps you look better. A good thing too, as the effects of the cell therapy, while longterm, are invisible. So, whether or not you leave Clinique La Prairie having bought yourself a few extra years or months in peak condition, it's an added bonus to know that you'll definitely come away looking both leaner and fitter.

Shambhala Spa, Parrot Cay, Turks and Caicos.

Shambhala Spa

T o most, the ideal holiday involves brilliant turquoise seas, crystalline sands and ever-present sunshine. While many places promise this ideal, few deliver. One that does is Parrot Cay, a 400-hectare private island in the midst of the Turks and Caicos archipelago.

Parrot Cay, a brief hour's flight from Miami, could not be more secluded and unspoilt. Nature lovers and paradise seekers alike will delight in its five kilometres of dazzlingly white sandy beaches, its unspoilt wetlands and mangrove swamps, the cactus groves, a kaleidoscope of marine life and more than 175 species of bird. Parrot Cay's isolation (it's a 40-minute boat ride from the main island of Providenciales), which once made it a perfect pirate's lair (parrot is derived from pirate), now make it the ideal place for the over-stressed to unwind.

The rooms are spacious, cool and airy, and are simply decorated in white muslins and plain woods. There are large four-poster beds, hammocks on the terraces and vast sofas on the verandas. The main reception, lounge and bar area has a ceiling as high as a white mini-cathedral, and offers great views sweeping down to the ocean.

A little to one side of the main hotel, hidden among trees and overlooking the lagoon, are the three simple wooden pavilions that house the Shambhala Spa. Here ancient Asian disciplines and philosophies meet natural therapies; and elements of sea and earth are mixed with state-of-the-art Western know-how. The main pavilion is where most of the therapy suites are housed, each with its own Japanese bath and porch. On a lower level you will find saunas, a steam room and sun-deck with a large open-air infinity pool. Nearby is the movement pavilion, where daily fitness, stretching, yoga and pilates classes take place. The spa's pièce de résistance, however, is the Shambhala cottage, a private pavilion with a double treatment room, meditation and yoga area, and a private steam room. The cottage can be booked for just a few hours or the whole day, so treatments undergone within its wooden walls can be enjoyed in complete privacy. A further two smaller spa cottages are adjacent.

Yoga, meditation and balanced diet are at the heart of the Shambhala philosophy. Daily classes are open to all who wish to participate, and private lessons are also available. Deep, controlled

Peace and tranquillity are vital in helping calm over-stressed minds and relax over-tense bodies.

breathing is a great way to relieve stress, and classes in the discipline encourage guests to become more aware of its potential for release. Three or four times a year, special week-long retreats are organised for small specialist groups. One such workshop is dedicated to Jivamukti yoga, which blends asanas, music, meditation and relaxation. Jivamukti has been taken up with enthusiasm in Manhattan, and celebrities like Sting and Christy Turlington are ardent advocates. Teachers from their New York yoga centre visit Parrot Cay for the week-long programme, which includes at least four hours of instruction every day.

Then there are the treatments, most of which use Shambhala's own specially blended powders, lotions and oils, made from such ingredients as clove, sandalwood, lime and ginger. There are massages of every type including tuina. Tuina is part of the repertoire of traditional Chinese medicine, as much a part of any healing process as acupuncture and herbalism. It is little known in the West, due to the years of study each practitioner must undergo, but its effect on the body when done well is invigorating, although the mix of pummelling, pulling and pinching it is not for the faint-hearted. The spa's signature massage, however, is the Shambhala, one of the most relaxing ever. It's a mix of Indonesian and Indian techniques – the first intense and deep, the latter more gentle – in tandem they're an almost ideal therapy for the stressed. The final knock-out is delivered by the spa's own specially blended oils.

Given that there's nothing to do but relax, and nowhere to go but another perfect beach with clear turquoise seas, time spent at Parrot Cay seems to pass all too quickly. There's an indolent magic to the place, which is why it's vital to have just one more Shambhala massage, attend one more yoga class or enjoy one more wrap before you suddenly discover that it's time to leave.

Thalassa Spa, Anassa, Cyprus.

Anassa

A ccording to estate agents, there are only three things that matter: location, location and location. Anassa, situated on Cyprus's northern coast, has all three. From its location on the pristine Asprokemnos beach, it is the ideal setting for those who want to get away from it all, yet it is still within easy reach of a town – Paphos, the birthplace of Aphrodite is a scant 40 minutes' drive away, while the tiny village of Polis is within walking distance. The hotel is built to resemble a traditional Byzantine village, complete with whitewashed walls, clay tiles, a village square and private chapel, Ayia Athanasia. The grounds are a riot of colour, blazing with bougainvillaea, hibiscus, lavender and plumbago.

Anassa's interior features natural materials – cottons, linens, cane and wood – all in a palette of neutral shades and pastel tones. Scattered throughout the hotel are mosaics, statues, frescoes, reliefs and motifs that speak eloquently of Cyprus's Roman, Greek and Venetian heritage. Most of the rooms and suites are in the main building, although a few are dotted around the gardens. Those who want to enjoy complete privacy and yet benefit from all the amenities of a five-star hotel can choose to stay in the Alexandros residence, a secluded two-bedroomed villa that comes complete with its own swimming pool and terrace.

Thalassa, Anassa's luxury spa, is situated next to the tiny church in the main square of the hotel complex. Named in honour of – and inspired by – marine therapies (thalassotherapy – thalassa – the Greek word for sea and therapia, Greek for treatment), the spa offers a huge range of seawater treatments as well as those based on marine algae and mud. Rather unusually, it also offers therapies that use purified sand from the beaches as a gentle exfoliant. In all the thalassotherapy treatments, water is pumped from the sea and heated to various temperatures in order to activate positive ions, which are believed to help regenerate and improve circulation and cell renewal.

In particular, Anassa features a virtual flood of thalassotherapy treatments that incorporate seaweed. These range from the straightforward and rather gentle thalasso bath to the bath with underwater massage, where a number of pressurised jets are used to massage muscles and joints. I'd recommend topping the

The traditional colours of Cyprus – brilliant white, shades of terracotta and the bright blue of sea and sky – are all incorporated into the décor of the resort.

Elegant terraces and walkways, areas of
shade and calm, all underline Anassa's
easy elegance.

treatment off with an exfoliation that uses marine algae to enhance the release of tension. There's a complete affusion shower treatment, in which numerous gentle jets of water are directed all over the body from all angles to stimulate the circulation, helping to pump oxygen around the body, thus relieving stress and revitalising the skin.

A much fiercer version of this – and, without a doubt, my favourite thalassotherapy treatment – is known as the complete thalasso jet shower at Anassa. Other places I've been to call it the grande douche or the jet blitz. In it, the therapist stands at one end of a long tiled room with a high-pressure hose while you stand stark naked at the other end. The treatment begins slowly and at a reasonably low pressure as each area of the body is massaged in turn with warm water. It hurts – but it's a good kind of hurt, and it works, invigorating and toning your muscles, especially if you request increased pressure – although it does feel as if you're going 10 rounds with the French riot police. The really brave finish the treatment with an icy blast of marine water. Thanks to its intensity, the treatment is short, no more than 12-15 minutes at a time; after it's over, guests are cocooned in warm towels and blankets and taken to the relaxation area to recuperate for a further quarter of an hour. Just three or four such treatments gives results – you can actually feel your body tightening up and the excess centimetres disappearing.

Thalassa also offers much gentler treatments that include aromatherapy massages, a choice of ayurvedic treatments as well as reflexology and reiki. There's also a whole host of facials, scrubs and polishes, alongside a special bust-firming therapy. One of Anassa's strong points is its range of pre-natal treatments, all specially devised to help the mother-to-be achieve a blissed-out state of comfort and relaxation.

Once you have been bathed, pummelled and massaged with elements and gifts of the sea, perhaps it will be time to set off for the real thing and simply enjoy the beach.

Mandara Spa

The Bahamas were obviously invented for sybarites – 700 islands, scattered with silver sands, set in warm turquoise seas and dotted with palm trees and sprinkled recklessly between the tip of Florida and the northernmost reaches of the main Caribbean islands. Not to mention the endless sunshine. Hardly surprising, then, that one of these islands ended up being called Paradise Island – or that paradise has become home to the Ocean Club, a former private estate that was developed in the 1960s by the American socialite and mega-millionaire Huntington Hartford, a man who clearly did not understand the meaning of the word excess.

First a 12th-century Augustinian cloister was reconstructed piecemeal from the remnants of a European original in the grounds, while the gardens themselves were modelled on those of Versailles. Its glories were allowed to fade for a while but, over the past 10 years, the place has been restored, refurbished and revamped.

There's a championship golf course, several tennis courts and watersports of all descriptions, as well as a casino at the club's sister resort Atlantis. But Ocean Club is also home to one of the few Mandara spas outside Asia – reason enough for giving everything else on offer a miss. At Ocean Club treatments take place in exquisite Balinese villas, each with their own private garden, waterfall shower and whirlpool bath.

While many of the treatments come straight from the Mandara textbook, a number have been specially adapted to incorporate some of the Caribbean's native ingredients and traditions. The Caribbean awakening is a good example of the Mandara's successful mix of traditions: the invigorating Caribbean coffee body scrub uses a blend of finely ground, locally grown coffee and tiny particles of volcanic pumice stone from Bali's holy mountains to gently abrade skin to polished perfection.

But massage is what the spa excels at – and a wide choice is on the menu. There's traditional Swedish, in which the manipulation of your body assists lymphatic drainage, improves circulation and soothes frayed muscles. Then there's the special sports massage, designed to increase flexibility and relieve tightness in those areas most used by golfers, tennis players or windsurfers. The royal Thai version is great for stretching, restoring suppleness and realigning

Light, space and fresh ocean air – all help achieve a sense of well-being.

the body and its internal organs; the aroma stone uses hot stones placed on energy points to warm your muscles before the massage begins in earnest; and yet others aim to relax every bit of the body. However if you are dithery – and greedy – like me and cannot make up your mind (or want them all), go for the Ocean Club special. For 180 minutes you'll have the undivided attention of two therapists, who run the whole gamut of international massage in a treatment that combines the best of shiatsu and its manipulation of the pressure points, the stretching elements of Thai, the great rolling strokes of lomi lomi from Hawaii, the muscular manoeuverings of the Swedish and the intense pummelling of the Balinese variety. After all the pummelling you feel a bit like a rag doll, so take time to recover with one of the special herbal teas.

Other treatments include the delicious-sounding strawberry herbal back cleanse (it smells pretty good too), while the Elemis soothing sunburn treatment borrows from Tahitian remedies that use frangipani and coconut to soothe skin that has been exposed to the sun too long. One of the newer and more popular treatments is the Fennel cleansing and colon therapy, which is prescribed for cellulite. First a detoxifying fennel and birch peel-off body mask is combined with particular massage techniques that target the hips and thighs to boost blood flow and help drain excess fluid away, then the stomach and digestive tract area around the abdomen is massaged and finally a spot of reflexology helps release blocked areas. The spa suggests that two treatments should be taken over a five-day period for the best results.

Once you've had enough of the heavenly delights of paradise, head for the Ocean Club's larger, brasher sister resort Atlantis – so called because it is in part a recreation of the lost city of Atlantis – a short shuttle ride away. Its nine swimming pools, 20 restaurants, flood-lit tennis courts and casino are a temptation even for those with the purest of intentions.

The Spa at the Westin Turnberry Resort, Ayershire, Scotland.

Turnberry

The he west coast of Scotland boasts some of the most magnificent scenery in Europe: great craggy rock faces, wild mountains, tiny coves, dramatic inlets, ruined castles and windswept islands. On a wintry day it can look almost forbidding, albeit unforgettable; but, when the sun shines and its rays hit the sea and the glens, it comes pretty close to heaven on earth. Turnberry, perched on the edge of the Ayrshire coastline, at the southern extreme of this stunning natural backdrop, began life during the Edwardian boom as one of the UK's great railway hotels. Set in 325 hectares of magnificent parkland, the hotel is linked to the coastline by two championship golf courses, the Ailsa and the Kintyre. The latter overlooks the Isle of Arran, which sparkles in the distance like an uncut gem; while the Ailsa, which has hosted the British Open on three occasions, is ranked among the world's best and exerts a magnetic pull on keen golfers from all parts of Europe, Asia and the USA.

The hotel's spa was built in the early 1990s to relieve the aching muscles of tired golfers and to cosset the hundreds of golf widows who accompany them to the bracing Ayrshire coast every year. It stands to one side of the hotel and houses a dozen treatment rooms, saunas, steam rooms and a 20 metre glass-walled swimming pool with views out across the Irish Sea to the lighthouse at Ailsa Craig.

Because of its proximity to the sea, many of the spa's treatments incorporate marine salts, algae and seaweeds – and you can buy all of the bath and body products to use at home. These include marine salts, good for body toning; a contouring seaweed bath essence that helps to continue the detoxification process back in your own bathroom; and a seaweed body gel. The hydrotherapeutic treatments offered by the spa are particularly effective in dealing with poor circulation – by boosting the flow of blood and oxygen around the body, water massages can help to clear some of the body's toxins and combat water retention. If you're after pampering, rather than deep cleansing, indulge in a multi-jet bath in warm water during which the jets massage you from the soles of your feet to the nape of your neck. At Turnberry they add various seaweeds or salts to the water, depending on whether you need to relax or detox. The gentle hissing of the water, the dimmed lights and the cocooning warmth

combine to turn this treatment into one of the most soporific I've ever experienced.

But if you want to get a real taste (and smell) of Turnberry, opt for the full-body algae or mud mask – the algae is the more revitalising of the two, while the somewhat more pungent mud soothes both body and mind. First your body is gently brushed and exfoliated, then a warm algae gel or mud paste is spread all over your body and you're wrapped in a type of clingfilm that keeps the heat in, helping you to sweat out any impurities. Once you're totally immobilised, you're placed under infra-red lamps to turn up the heat, aiding the absorption of the minerals and enzymes in the mud or algae. This is another Turnberry soporific special – I don't know of anybody who's ever managed to stay awake during this part of the treatment. Once you're 'cooked', the mask is showered off, leaving you completely relaxed with soft, silky skin.

Turnberry's other specialities include a great deep-cleansing back treatment; a face and back treatment that cleanses, tones, exfoliates and rehydrates; and a golfer's package that features a hydrotherapy bath and a back, neck and shoulder massage, as well as a foot treatment – something for every part of the body used in the game. Other packages include a complete top-to-toe pampering that ends with a session with the hairdresser and an anti-stress / anti-jetlag programme that begins with the hydrotherapy bath followed by three stress-relieving treatments for face, body and scalp.

Of them all, though, I have to admit that my favourite is the 90-minute holistic special for face, scalp and back. It refines my skin, eases my tired muscles and relaxes my mind. After it ends, I enjoy nothing better than heading outside, refreshed and invigorated, for a good long walk along that breathtaking coastline in the bracing Ayrshire wind.

Les Thermes Marins de Monte Carlo, Monaco.

Les
Thermes
Marins

A tiny principality, just two kilometres square, wedged between France and Italy, Monte Carlo is well known for its casinos, its royal family – the Grimaldis, whose crop of princes and princesses both fascinate and shock the rest of Europe, its Grand Prix and its population of tax exiles. In addition to any number of gilded casinos and high-rise millionaires' mansions, Monaco, the principality's only city, is also home to one of Europe's best resorts. Founded in 1863 by Prince Charles III, the Société des Bains de Mer is a unique complex made up of four luxury hotels, an opera house, casino, several Michelin-starred restaurants and a world-class spa, Les Thermes Marins.

The spa's reputation has been built on the strength of its thalassotherapy treatments. The ancient Greeks were the first to recognise the potential therapeutic benefits of seawater and its algae and seaweeds. The word itself is derived from the Greek *thalassa* – sea, and *therapeia* – treatment. A true thalassotherapy spa should use unpolluted seawater pumped directly from the sea. At Les Thermes Marins, the water is pumped in from 300 metres offshore and a depth of 37 metres to ensure maximum purity and the highest concentration of mineral salts, algae, marine mud and iodine, then heated to body temperature before being used in treatments. Its effectiveness is due to the fact that the minerals and trace elements found in such pure seawater are almost identical to those found in the body's fluids, making absorption easier.

Among the range of thalassotherapy treatments offered here is the ultra-relaxing hydromassage, in which a pressure-adjustable hose is played over your body as you float in a warm bath of seawater. There's also the affusion massage, in which a relaxing spray of warm seawater is combined with a hand massage that uses lubricating essential oils – an invigorating jet shower that targets a stream of seawater onto specific parts of the body before a deep tissue massage is performed by hand; this is great for breaking up fatty cells, boosting circulation and combating cellulite. Also on offer are algae and mud packs, which draw out the body's toxins and soften the skin, and a number of baths that combine essential

oils with the purified seawater for a super-relaxing effect.

Most thalassotherapy spas prescribe a course of treatments for guests and Les Thermes Marins is no exception, advising a minimum stay of six days for the azur tonic, also known here as the 'complete cure'. Other packages and programmes are also available – these can take anything from one day to a week to complete. Some of these incorporate beauty treatments at a dedicated centre, Le Salon Bleu, while others are devoted to weight loss and stress control.

The phlebological exercises are another of the spa's exclusive treatments. Designed specifically to deal with heavy or painful legs, water retention and swollen ankles, the exercises are performed in cool seawater, which stimulates the flow of both blood and lymph. At the same time, the arches of your feet are massaged as you walk over a pebble-strewn surface – although somewhat painful at first, after a few passes over the smooth stones you'll find yourself actually enjoying the sensation. An invigorating jet of water massages your legs at the same time. By the end of a session, you'll feel like you're walking on air.

Treatments at Le Salon Bleu include a wide range of facials – deep moisturising, anti-ageing, lifting – as well as a number of peels. Products are used containing glycolic acid which gently peels away the top layer of skin to reveal the newer, brighter cells beneath; or there's the salon's exclusive sea peel, which is based on salt taken from the Dead Sea and mixed with a blend of essential oils specially tailored to the needs of your skin. It has a fantastic refining, softening effect – even wrinkles don't seem so prominent afterwards – I recommend it highly. Make sure you test a patch of skin beforehand, though, as some people don't react well to the treatment.

Traditionally, Monte Carlo has been both home and play-ground to millionaires from around the world, but you, too, can get that million-dollar feeling after one short trip to Les Thermes Marins de Monte Carlo.

Exotic

Different
Glamorous
Striking
Strange
Outré

Exotic is a word made for spas. In every way they are a different experience in different places. They take us away from the ordinary, the humdrum, the prosaic. Spas offer the feel-good, feel-a-whole-lot better factor. Where else could you have a Balinese wrap in Brussels or a shiatsu massage in Saratoga but in a spa.

Exotic is as far away from everyday life as can be. It is why people are flocking to spas for a taste and an experience of something glamorous and mysterious. This begins with the décor often a mix of silks and voiles, of sheen and transparency where fantasy and reality merge. Add to that, the scent assault of everything from ginger to jasmine, to candles and incense sticks, the sounds of Tibetan bells and the sights of floating frangipani petals and mounds of volcanic rock, and we are as far away from real life as we want to be. And there are the crystals, the springs and the waters for healing and bathing. Then take into account the muds and salts, the marine algae, the herbal extracts, the fruit pulps and the floral essences — all of which are used in treatments, and welcome how the earth has given of its riches for our sense of well-being. What could be more exotic?

Las Ventanas al Paraiso

Mosaics, local plants and stones give a
sense of opulent exoticism to one of
Mexico's premier spas.

Baja California is how this area is officially designated. A spit of land which surges south from the state and yet is as Mexican as it is possible to be. A land of desert and wilderness with huge rock formations and some of the most spectacular Pacific seascapes. A peninsula which separates the calm Sea of Cortez from the wild excesses of the aforementioned ocean – and at its very tip are the windows to paradise – Las Ventanas al Paraiso.

It is the sign of a serious and confident spa that treatments and therapies are constantly re-evaluated while research continues for new and effective ones. The Spa at Las Ventanas al Paraiso is such a place where nothing is left to chance and yet everything seems so effortless. The hotel is a mix of Mexican and Mediterranean where white painted houses of differing sizes and heights are broken up with narrow pebbled paths, wide piazzas with fountains and statues, bougainvillaea teaming over walls and water everywhere from the aforementioned fountains, infinity swimming pools and everywhere the sight and sound of the crashing surf of the Sea of Cortez. In between all of this are cool and shady areas for eating, shopping, relaxing and supping. Throughout are examples of Mexican arts and crafts from the huge blue zigzag decoration on white ceramic pots to the embroidered cushions and hangings, from the Conchuela stone floors in which fossilised sea shells can be found to the pebble decorated paths and bedheads.

To one side, overlooking the ocean is the Robert Trent Jones golf course while in a quiet corner part of, yet apart from, the main hotel area is The Spa. On two levels it houses a gym and fitness area, four treatment rooms with exquisitely painted ceilings, an outdoor relaxation area complete with fountain, a sauna, steam room, splash pool and whirlpool as well as four exquisite self-contained treatment suites. These have both an indoor and an outdoor treatment area – the latter in a shaded area overlooking a Zen-like desert garden planted with cacti of different species and heights in carefully raked sand. Separate entrances for men and women lead to individual preparation areas, which are scented with eucalyptus and where everything from fruit juices to robes and slippers are presented. Guests can of course, eschew these suites and instead opt to have their treatments in their own suite, or in the beach pavilion

where only the sound of the waves accompanies the massage and manipulation or for a real escape from reality choose 'the Yenecamu' (local Pericu Indian word meaning a place between two waters). This involves heading off into the ocean or the Sea of Cortez in the Las Ventanas 55 foot yacht, the Gin, for two hours of face and body wraps plus a massage for two all on board.

And then there are the treatments – more than 60 of them emanating from all around the globe. From Mexico there are treatments using desert clay which was first used by the Mayans and Aztecs millennia ago) which, rich in minerals, is used to detoxify and exfoliate while the bark from the local Tepezcohuite plant is mixed with cream and rose water and used to rehydrate dry and sun burned skin, while a gel from another local plant, the nopal, is applied to the body to help eliminate toxins and water retention from the body. The special wrap using it is concluded with a delicious smoothie made from pineapple and nopal!

One of the very newest treatments, and additions take place all the time, is the fantastic Raindrop therapy where nine different oils are sprinkled along the spine. These are basil, cypress, marjoram, oregano, peppermint, thyme, wintergreen plus two blends which also include such ingredients as rosewood and frankincense as well as spruce and lavender! Each oil is sprinkled individually before being massaged along the spine and when all nine have been used, the massage strokes are combined with a type of Tibetan reflexology (Vita Flex), all to help release muscle tension and spasms as well as helping boost the body's immune system. Well, from one who has tried it, let me say it also induces near-coma relaxation. Not to be missed. Another great treatment is the scalp and reflexology combo, which concentrates on the two extremities – head and feet. You will feel light as air afterwards while your hair will have been given a great conditioning treatment with neem oil before being wrapped in a warm towel.

And all the time the waves thunder by. When you emerge from the cocoon of the spa it is the first thing you hear, when you open your French windows in the morning it is the same sound that greets you, and it is the sound that sends you to sleep. One of the best stress busters ever is the sound of the waves, and here it is all around you.

Sun, sand and seawater are vital to this Mexican experience – as is the scent of eucalyptus throughout.

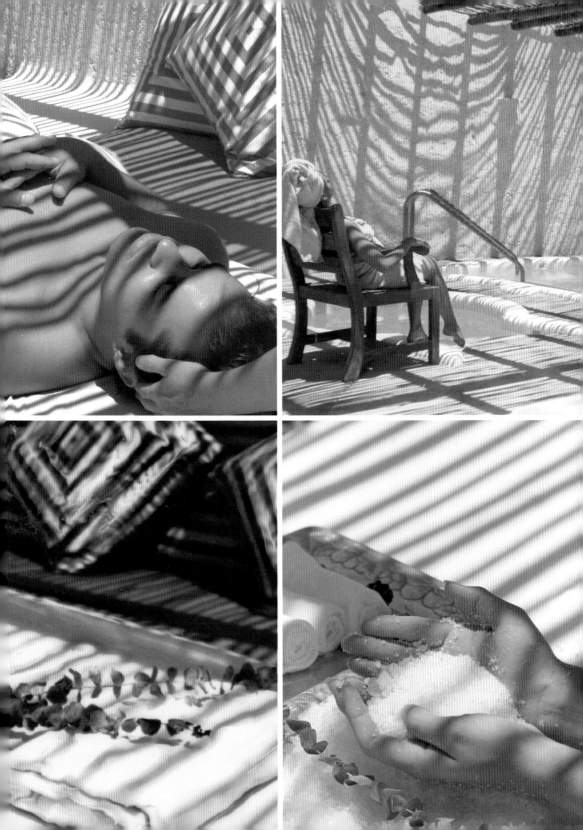

Amanjena

A city of medieval souks, sunset-hued walls and lush gardens, Marrakesh is exotic, mysterious and utterly glamorous. At its epicentre stands the Djemma el Fna, an open square where snake charmers, fortune-tellers and water-sellers ply their trade, story -tellers weave their sibilant magic and traders tout goods from embroidered slippers to CDs.

While Marrakesh itself is a confusion of cacophony and crowds, those seeking calm and solitude will find it at Amanjena, whose name means peaceful paradise, a few miles out of town. At first sight all you see are the high walls made of ochre pisé – a traditional mixture of red earth and straw – that surround traditional Moroccan villages. Once through the gates, though, you enter a different world, a universe of fountains, courtyards and colonnades. At its centre lies a traditional irrigation pool, which, in this arid environment, feels like an oasis in the middle of the desert. The cooling effect is enhanced by a huge swimming pool set in a vast colonnaded square. Beyond these lie the hotel's wonderfully formal gardens, where canals trickle past stylised, geometric parterres.

Paths radiate out from here and lead to the pavilions (Amanjena has no rooms, as such). Each has a huge domed living area, warmed by an open fireplace, while out in the private courtyards, or menzahs, are fountains and a canopied bath. No wonder so many guests choose to enjoy treatments in the privacy of their own pavilions. If you require even more luxury, you can opt for one of six two-storey maisons, each with its own private pool and butler. In both pavilions and maisons, the decorative theme is inspired by the location, from the hand-crafted furniture, ironwork and rugs – great splashes of Berber reds and saffrons –to the leather chairs and cushions.

The spa itself is on the other side of the pool from the pavilions, through vast wooden doors that lead through long marble corridors into a haven of peace and cool. There are high-ceilinged treatment rooms, a whirlpool, a sauna and two traditional hammams (one for men, the other for women), exquisitely tiled in shades of green. A small but tailored menu of treatments is on offer – all using local spices and essential oils (Morocco is particularly famed for its rose oil). Traditional methods have been combined with the latest research

to create the spa's beauty treatments. In particular, its facials, cleansings, masks and manicures were devised by French beauty guru, Anne Semonin. Her ultra-exclusive products, which blend the purest of essential oils with plant and algal essences, are highly sought after, and Amanjena is one of the few places you'll find them outside France. The facials, in particular, are excellent – good for all skin types, but simply fantastic for dry, mature skins. Whichever you opt for, you're in luck. French-trained beauticians invariably give the best facials: they pummel your skin to get your circulation going and give you a healthy glow, search keenly for well-hidden blackheads and whiteheads, which they extract with supreme efficiency, cleanse thoroughly and tidy up your brows as they go. Definitely an experience not to be missed.

While you're there, you should also try the traditional Moroccan gommage, a hammam treatment that begins with a steam session, quickly followed by an application of the spa's own savon noir (black olive soap), which in turn is followed by what can only be described as an energetic scrub with a sort of loofah mitt. The suds are rinsed away before your head and hair is washed energetically. The whole experience is topped off with the application of either a henna or a clay rinse, depending on your type of hair and scalp. Finally, once every part of you is sluiced and rinsed, you are wrapped in thick towels and given delicious mint tea to sip.

Another option is the spa's exclusive Moroccan massage, which uses argan oil to lubricate the long, deep strokes. This deliciously nutty-smelling oil is made from the fruit of the Arganias spinosa tree, which is native to Essaouira, a couple of hours away from Marrakesh towards the coast. The oil is also used in the preparation of food, mainly as a garnish for salads and dips, and is seldom seen outside Morocco. You can, of course, find it in the city's labyrinthine souk, but do remember to take a guide as it's easy to get lost in the twists and turns of its alleyways. A guide can also help you save both time and money on your shopping. Whatever you're after, whether it's rugs, metalwork, antiques or djellabahs and babouches, the guide will know where to find the best examples at the most reasonable prices, speeding up the whole process and hastening your return to the tranquillity of Amanjena.

Mauna Lani, Hawaii, USA.

Mauna
Lani

Hawaii's dramatic landscape is built of once molten rock, carved and sculpted into mountains whose wooded slopes rise steeply from the Pacific waters. Mauna Lani Spa, at the epicentre of the 500-year-old Kaniku lava flow, whose wide expanses are dotted with spring-fed pools, couldn't be better situated to evoke the islands' volcanic magnificence. The spa's theme of fire and ice is a reflection of the geological wonders for which the main island of Hawaii is known, from the snow-topped peaks of Mauna Kea to the still-flowing lava of Kilauea Crater. Because of its geothermal activity, the island has always been thought of as a healing centre, particularly the northern part of the island, whose heart is the piko (centre) of five mountains.

Everything at Mauna Lani, from its architecture to the menu of treatments, has been inspired by the history, culture and mythology of the island. The indoor/outdoor spa offers everything from lava rock saunas to a traditional healing garden, a la'au, whose plants have been grown for centuries for their culinary, medical and beautifying properties. With its traditional thatched treatment hale (huts), the whole area is designed to resemble a local village. Two hale have lava rock soaking tubs, a third an outdoor Vichy shower. There are outdoor showers and plunge pools as well as a meditation pavilion elsewhere in the grounds. But the spa's pièce de résistance is its open-air, sun-warmed lava sauna, where a black clay mud treatment is applied before you detoxify in the sauna while waiting for the mud to dry. To maximise the benefits, you are offered melted ice to ladle over your body. Finally you rinse off in an outdoor garden shower – fire, ice, and a very refreshed you.

Although the whole area, designed to recreate a historical lava flow, looks more like a moonscape than anything else, the effect is softened by a fragrance garden in which more than 1,000 plants and flowers with aromatherapeutic properties have been planted. Therapists at the spa are trained to incorporate these into the lotions and oils they employ in the treatments and, if you want to find out more about the plants and their uses, they will give you a guided tour of the gardens. The spa's interior is almost as exotic as its exterior, with a wealth of local materials used in its building and decorations.

But it is the treatments, as ever, that define a spa. While Mauna Lani offers massages, hydrotherapy and facials sourced all around

The healing power of flowers is harnessed to those of fire, ice and water in this most dramatic of resorts.

the world, from Sweden to Thailand, the ones to choose are those that are firmly grounded in Hawaiian history. The traditional massage of Polynesia is the lomi lomi, in which the therapist uses his or her forearms and elbows (ouch) extensively in kneading out the tension. While lomi lomi is available in spas around the world, this is the place to have it. Pluck up courage and go for it – even though it's not the most comfortable sensation, lomi lomi is worth every moment of potential agony in terms of its ability to reinvigorate. If you are feeling wimpish, begin with a 30-minute version. After many years of massage, I have become so greedy for pain that I invariably opt for a full hour and a half of Polynesian torture.

In a touching ritual that sets the scene for all that is to come, massages at Mauna Lani begin with a pule or prayer. Tradition has been extended with the introduction of the spa's signature lomi lomi hula, in which the massage strokes are done in time to Hawaiian music. It's a strange feeling, a bit like having someone do the hula while standing on you. The advantage is that it is much softer than the traditional lomi lomi.

The Hawaiians have their own version of stone therapy, which uses the local basalt stones. Pohaku pa'a starts by heating the stones in a fire before they are placed along your spine – these heat your muscles, allowing the masseur to apply greater pressure, which results in a tremendous loosening of the muscles. The spa has revived the tradition, and enhances the experience with either coconut or kukui oils, which lubricate the stones as they move over your body. The coconut is key to many of the therapies and is used as a key ingredient in wraps, baths and scrubs, as is the locally grown ginger, which stimulates the circulation, while sea salt and seaweed are used to exfoliate and purify. One of the great detox treatments here is the icy glacier clay therapy. It's not as bad as it sounds – the white clay they use isn't freezing, it just comes from the glacier. Applied to the body in a thorough coat it helps lure impurities, toxins and excess fluids out of the body.

With its distinctive mix of hard volcanic and soft floral, Mauna Lani Spa is like nowhere else on earth. At once tough and sweet, fire and ice, it provides an absolutely unique experience.

The Pavilion Spa, Lizard Island, Northern Queensland, Australia.

Lizard Island

At the risk of being accused of spouting clichés, if there were a heaven on earth, I'd have to say it could possibly be found on Lizard Island. The most northerly of the islands along the tropical North Queensland coast, it basks in the sunshine right on top of the Great Barrier Reef, one of the wonders of the natural world. The island itself is a small, rocky outpost of civilisation in the middle of an expanse of azure ocean, and many of its 24 white sandy beaches are accessible only by boat. Although this is divers' paradise, you can witness awesome wonders just by putting on a snorkel mask – on a good day, the water's so clear you don't even need to bother with that, you just stand in the shallows and watch the fish flit past you. Still, should you decide to be more adventurous make a point of going to Cod Hole, where the fish are literally the size of German Shepherd dogs. Don't worry though, they don't bite.

Lizard is a dedicated national park and, if you can tear yourself away from the beach, it is worth walking through the bush to Cook's Look where, from a height of 350 metres, you can see nothing but the big blue sea. Considering it is less than 27 kilometres from the Queensland coast, Lizard feels like the most isolated place on earth.

The resort, although small (it only has 40 suites), offers plenty to do. There is a plethora of water sports, of course; deep-sea fishing, trips out to the reef and the opportunity to explore each and every one of those 24 magnificent beaches. And naturally like any hedonistic hideaway, Lizard has its very own spa – the Pavilion, a microcosm of ancient and modern, West and East. Given Lizard Island's geographical location, which puts it almost as close to Asia as it is to the great cities of Sydney and Melbourne, this part of Australia is as much influenced by Asian culture and customs as it is by the West. The Pavilion's aboriginal heritage is also evident in many of the ingredients used for wraps and scrubs. A treatment called promised time, for instance, evokes the aboriginal dreamtime through a careful choice of native ingredients. Salts, infused with lemon myrtle, are the main ingredients in a scrub that gently exfoliates your body. This is followed by a mud mask of pepper berry and peat, which is smoothed all over to warm your body and help it to rid itself of toxins and excess fluid. The names of the treatments are often as evocative as the ingredients. The delicious-

sounding lillypilly facial uses indigenous wattleseed and lemon myrtle to cleanse, then following it up with a Tasmanian kelp (similar to seaweed) mask that's used to help eliminate impurities and a thorough anointing with a macadamia moisturiser. In a rousingly Australian finale, you're given lemon myrtle tea to encourage you to relax even more.

Although the Pavilion only offers four different aromatherapy massages, a quick glance through the menu makes me dither for ages as I pin down my choice to just one of the magical-sounding options. There's peace, which uses a blend of lavender, camomile and geranium to perfume the oil; or love, a mix of rose, ylang-ylang, jasmine and sandalwood, I'm almost seduced by meditation, a potpourri of frankincense, myrrh, sandalwood and vetiver.

With more than a nod to the spa's Asian neighbours, the glorious two-hour green tea geisha, the fourth massage, is based on traditional Japanese treatments and is the one I would opt for. A mix of brown rice, sesame seeds, sea salt and green tea is used to slough off any dead cells and smooth the skin. It's followed by a wrap that has more than a touch of the herb garden to it and a mask made from a blend of camellia oil (good for cellulite), green tea, green clay and essential oils of cypress, juniper, lemon and sweet fennel, a combination that acts to rid the skin of impurities. Once it's rinsed off, bliss follows with a soothing but firm massage in which the lotion used contains a mix of green tea and citrus fruits, leaving you not just cleansed but soft and silky too.

Like I said, cliché though it might be, Lizard Island is heaven on earth for body, mind and spirit.

Attention to detail in décor, products and accessories is the hallmark of a serious spa.

Rajvilas, Jaipur, India.

Rajvilas

Possibly the most magnificent of all the Indian states, Rajasthan is vast and arid, yet rich in history and culture. Its name literally means 'land of the kings', those fierce yet glamorous Rajput princes and warriors whose legacy can be found in the great cities of the state – Jaipur, Jodphur, Udaipur and Jaisalmer.

As a result, Rajasthan is full of forts, palaces and royal hunting lodges in various stages of repair. It hardly needed another grand building, but that is exactly what happened when Rajvilas was built less than five years ago just kilometres from the centre of Jaipur. It is a perfect reconstruction of a 19th-century Rajasthani fort, a project that took 800 workers three years to build. Fifty skilled carvers were retained to produce more than 200 stone pillars and statues. With 54 deluxe rooms and 14 luxury tents, not to mention hectares of Mughal-style gardens, dotted about with moats, fountains and lotus ponds, the completed Rajvilas is almost beyond opulence.

The whole concept is a marriage of Mughal and Hindu influences. The main buildings, made of local stone, are encased in a pink lime plaster that imitates the sandstone used by the Mughal rulers in the construction of the forts of Delhi and Agra, while the interiors are washed in a creamy ivory araish – the traditional finish found in most Rajasthani palaces. Blue Jaipur tiles in shimmering shades of lapis, turquoise and ultramarine provide a thread that runs throughout the hotel's décor; alcoves are lined in gold leaf and dyes made by grinding semi-precious stones are used to decorate the cusped arches found in the hotel's public rooms. A team of craftsmen, headed by traditional master artist Ghanshyan Nimbark, was responsible for the elaborate frescoes in the main dining room, and the dangling crystal chandeliers conjure up echoes of the Raj.

Guest rooms are clustered in groups around courtyards decorated with fountains, tumbling greenery, blue-tiled walls and glorious frescoes. Inside you'll find embroidered hangings and throws, cotton dhurries, wicker baskets, and forged silver dishes and candlesticks. The most evocative rooms of all, however, are not rooms at all but vast tents, based on those used by the Rajput princes in their travels, tethered in their own desert-style encampment. En-suite bathrooms with roll-top baths, teak floors, shimmering silks, draped canopies and beautiful hand-blocked

fabrics by Franco-Indian designer Brigitte Singh come as standard.

To one side of the property, just beyond the peacocks and the swimming pool, is the restored haveli – a traditional merchant's house – that houses the spa. It bases its original treatments and philosophy on a mix of ayurveda and aromatherapy which it calls aromaveda, but still offers therapies from other cultures. The core treatments are based on non-clinical ayurvedic principles. The pure indulgence treatment is a three-part cleanser and moisturiser that begins with a rice and warm buttermilk exfoliation, follows it up with a rice- and herb-based refining treatment and ends with a moisturising massage.

Whatever you do, make sure you have an Indian head massage while you are at Rajvilas. It's incredibly stimulating – I can really feel the blood flowing around my head after a session – as well as being good for the scalp. At Rajvilas the massage is a fraction gentler than it might be elsewhere in India, but you can (I do) ask for it to be stronger. Although there are moments you fear your skull may be crushed, you feel fantastically invigorated afterwards. Mind you, you will look terrible afterwards – like a medusa. The only solution is to wrap a towel, turban-like, around your head and hotfoot it back to your room and shower.

No self-respecting Indian spa would be complete if it didn't offer a range of yoga and meditation classes. Taking a yoga class on the lawns outside the haveli is the highlight of any visit. The song of the birds and the splash of the fountains are the only things to impinge on the subconscious after a few minutes spent focusing on your breathing and posture. An hour or so of this will set you up nicely for a morning's sightseeing in the glorious city of Jaipur; although it's down to you whether you head first for the decorative riches of the Amber Fort or opt instead for the Palace of the Winds, from whose windows the ladies of the harem watched the world wander past. Perhaps you might decide to wander through the Jantar Mantar, an extraordinary architectural theme park built in 1728 to calculate the movements of the celestial bodies – its accuracy is awe-inspiring. Better still, visit all of them and then return to the bliss of an Indian head massage in the cool calm of the spa in the haveli.

A combination of ancient ayurvedic wisdom, traditional disciplines and modern research has been brought to bear on the treatments.

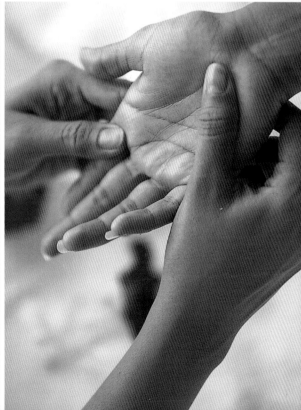

The Serenity Spa

Andalucia's history is one of the most colourful in Europe. As Spain's most southern province, it lies at the crossroads between Africa and Europe, the Atlantic and the Mediterranean. This location has always given the province huge strategic importance to conquerors, kings, merchants and sailors. You can still see traces of each successive wave of alien influence – the Romans and the Moors in particular, stamped their identity on this territory – most obviously in the fortresses, palaces and villages of the region. Its beauty, however, is also to be found in its dramatic scenery, glorious beaches, grand bullrings and the prettiest white washed villages in Spain. Hardly surprising then, that Andalucia is highly popular with tourists, most of whom head for the coast, which boasts more than 320 days of sunshine a year – a high quota for Europe. It is here right at the heart of the Costa del Sol that you find the Las Dunas Beach Hotel and Spa.

Built along the lines of the grandest Spanish hacienda, this flamingo pink establishment sits facing the beach, in the middle of hectares of tropical gardens strewn with pools and fountains. Even though it looks large, it houses just 73 rooms, all of which have their own private terrace or veranda and 33 luxury apartments. As if the hotel's extensive range of facilities, which include its bars, restaurants, a pool, water sports and beach activities, were not enough to induce a permanent state of well-being, guests can also make the most of the hotel's frescoed spa. The Serenity Spa, which offers treatments and therapies galore, is a place of repose and calm, redolent with the aroma of fragrant oils. If you're in need of a bit more than pampering, there's the Sol Kur-Clinic, run by Drs Hans and Rosemary Berneth, who specialise in both traditional and complementary medicine. Here, full medical examinations and fitness assessments are available, as well as physiotherapy, colonic treatments, AHA facials, which use fruit acids to help gently exfoliate skin, and collagen specials.

The spa's treatments have been specifically designed to use natural ingredients from both land and sea. The special ocean wrap, for instance, is a warm seaweed mask for the whole body. After it has been spread onto your skin, you're wrapped, first in clingfilm, then in a heavy blanket, so that the seaweed's active ingredients can get to work on eliminating toxins. While the heat and the minerals are working on your body, you get treated to a head and scalp massage and, to finish, you are showered off and a softening lotion is applied to your skin. The head and scalp massage uses a fair bit of oil – and, while you might recoil at the concept, my advice would be to go for it. Oily hair might feel strange – and look worse – but it's a great way of restoring some balance to your locks, particularly if you've spent a few days exposing it to sun and sea. Just comb your hair back at the end and pop on a sun hat, leaving the oil to do its stuff for a few hours.

Land-based treatments include an exotic coconut rub and milk wrap, which is a gentle but effective exfoliant, and a gloriously fragrant frangipani body wrap in which your skin is drenched with the scented oil before being cocooned in fluffy towels. To give your tan a boost you could always try the special ceremony of the sun, which begins with a body brushing, followed by a lime and ginger scrub and polish and ends with an application of self-tanning cream. The result? A golden tan without the ageing effect of the sun's rays. Or why not go the whole hog and spoil yourself with the special two-and-a-half-hour oriental serenity experience? Put your mind into neutral and your body into the capable hands of the therapists. First comes a lime and ginger salt glow – a wonderful mix of stimulating ginger and cleansing lime mixed with exfoliating sea salt. Then, get ready for a seriously relaxing aromatherapy massage: you can choose your favourite scent from a range of ready-mixed oils that include one for de-stressing, another for easing aching muscles, another for rebalancing mind and body and, finally, one for detoxing. My olfactory organs, for some reason always unerringly choose the stress-a-way. After an hour and a quarter of this pampering, your body feels like putty and is ready for the final part which you'll revel in – the sole delight, a super luxurious foot treatment, in which your feet are exfoliated, massaged, creamed and oiled. Walking on air is the only way to describe how you feel afterwards. That is, if you are up to walking.

Ancient practices combine with modern technology for a true spa experience.

The Veyoge Spa, Kanuhura Resort and Spa, Maldives.

The Veyoge Spa

People talk about the Maldives as if they were one particular place rather than a loose agglomeration of 1,192 islands and atolls. Together, they make up an extraordinary republic that floats just above the equator, southwest of India and to the west of Sri Lanka. Composed of coral, the atolls (the word comes from the Maldivian atolu) are situated on the peaks of an ancient sunken volcanic range. Only 200 or so are inhabited, of which a mere 86 are open to visitors. Some islands are little more than 10 metres long, none rise more than three metres above sea level. As well as being exquisite tropical hideaways with powdery white sands and warm cobalt seas, many atolls have recently been threatened by the rising sea levels of global warming, making them doubly precious. Most are protected by coral reefs, and the Maldives have become known as a divers' paradise, visitors flocking from far and wide to strap on tank and stare in wonderment at the vivid underwater world. The idle can simply lie on the surface of the water and snorkel.

Over the past 30 years a number of luxurious hotels have been built on the islands with the aim of providing the ideal get-away-from-it-all holiday for the really stressed and honeymooners in search of the trip of a lifetime. The latest of these pleasure domes is the Kanuhura Resort and Spa, which lies on the eastern edge of the practically untouched Lhaviyani atoll – some three-quarters of an hour by seaplane from the main airport on Male. The seaplane ride itself is reason enough for visiting the island – it skims over brilliant turquoise seas, swoops over deserted beaches and soars above hundreds of tiny palm-fringed islands on its way to its destination.

By the time you emerge from the plane you are already in island happy mode, and total relaxation is just a nanosecond away. So to help it on its way, head straight for the glories of the Veyoge Spa, which describes itself as the largest health and beauty centre in the Maldives. Its menu is a sophisticated amalgam of East and West, with massages from Sweden offered alongside the manawa massage of Polynesia, and reflexology from China on the menu next to Japanese silk facials. Local native healing oils are used in the traditional Maldivian theyo demun massage, which is quite a vigorous treatment incorporating short, firm strokes, strong manipulation of the pressure points and a deep scalp massage.

Far from the madding crowd – the sheer isolationist splendour of the island is an instant de-stressor.

It might seem a little strong to begin with, but after a few minutes you can feel the blood flow increase and some of those terrible knots in your muscles and joints begin to fade away. One of the most popular of all treatments is the aroma stone therapy. The smooth, flat stones come from river beds and are believed by native Americans to be filled with the energy of the water that flowed over them. This vitality unblocks the body's energies, which is why some stones are placed on key energy points before others are heated and smoothed with oil and used to massage the rest of your body.

Given that the spa is in the tropics, many of the cleansers, wraps and scrubs contain ingredients that reflect its location. There is papaya, coconut and frangipani on the menu, as well as vanilla and ginger. The exotic lime and ginger salt glow is used to cleanse and exfoliate the body to provide the perfect base for an even suntan. If you've had just a bit too much sun, book a cooling body soother treatment – a body mask composed of cucumber, yoghurt and mint is spread all over your body before it is wrapped in cellophane to bring all the toxins out of your pores. Cucumber slices are then placed over your face and your extremities – both feet and scalp – are massaged. It's the ultimate in refreshment after a draining day in the sun. Tired and dry skins will benefit from the Japanese silk booster facial, which incorporates silk protein among ingredients that replenish and rehydrate the skin – it's good, too, for mature skin. But the best facial of them all is the herbal lavender repair. It's partly to do with the divine aromas of lavender, thyme and rosemary that permeate the pavilion, a sensualist's delight, but it's also a great cleanser. Along with these traditional spa ingredients is Jurlique, line marketed as the 'Purest Skin Care on Earth'. Developed by German-Australians, Drs Jürgen and Ulrike Klein, it is based on the centuries-old arts of homeopathy, aromatherapy and alchemy.

I also enjoy the Thai foot ritual, a stretching pressure-point massage, which begins the whole treatment. It really does prove the old adage that if your feet hurt, it shows in your face – after a brief minute of rubbing, pulling and prodding, my frown lines begin to ease.

Of course the real benefit of island life, Kanuhura-style, is that everything is so laid back and relaxed that it will be some time before those frown lines reappear.

The Aroma Boma, Ulusaba, Sabi Sand Reserve, South Africa.

Ulusaba

There is something both mystical and magical about African mornings. The night is over and the survivors shake off the signs of battle and return to the bush and to their hides while the sun rises in its relentless circle of heat and light. For visitors it's the time to marvel at the dawn and head off to spot the lion and the elephant, the giraffe and the antelope as they retire into the infinite space and cover of Africa, it's when the jackal and the vulture pick clean the carcases left by the rulers of the jungle, its when Africa is at its most elemental – and its most beautiful. Forego the drive one morning and go on a walking safari instead where you can almost feel the heartbeat of Africa under your feet, and where you can observe plant, bird and insect life at close quarters.

One of the most luxurious places to enjoy the space and light of Africa is at Ulusaba, a private game park built into a rock formation on the western side of the Sabi-Sand Reserve. Here, the big five – elephant, lion, buffalo, rhino and leopard – roam freely across the invisible border between the Sabi-Sand and the adjacent Kruger National Park. Although the bush itself is a little on the wild side, the comforts of Ulusaba would not be out of place in the centre of a cosmopolitan city. There are just 20 rooms here – 10 in Rock Lodge and another 10 in Safari Lodge. The former is carved into the great cliff-face of Ulusaba itself and commands sweeping views from its position several hundred metres above the savannah. Safari Lodge, on the other hand, was built under the shady canopy of a cluster of ancient trees. Its rooms, which are decorated in traditional native colours, are resplendent with African weavings and carvings.

One of the best ways to recover after the rigours and stimulation of an early-morning game drive is to surrender yourself to one of the treatments on offer at the Aroma Boma. Most treatments are carried out in the Aroma Boma although it is possible to have them in the privacy of your room or on the sundeck of your lodge's swimming pool. There's a great hand zone treatment, a type of reflexology for the hand in which the pressure points are manipulated to release tensions and improve circulation. This is ecstasy, especially after a couple of hours spent gripping onto the rail of a Land Rover with one hand as you clutch your binoculars with the other. The really hedonistic will enjoy the full back-up massage – all you have to do

Sophistication in the wilderness – soft

towels, scented oils, total comfort.

is straddle the special chair while the therapist administers a very thorough pressure-point massage. You don't even have to remove your T-shirt or safari gear. For something a little more taxing there are a number of chiropractic treatments to choose from, including a deep-tissue massage.

Those who are into serious pampering will probably make a beeline for one of the specials – treatments to help Western skins deal with the after-effects of the merciless African sun. Even when you're protected by a hat and maximum-strength sunblock, it's virtually impossible to escape the sun's damaging rays. If you've overdone it, a soothing, healing face massage is the perfect antidote as it helps replenish the skin's moisture content. Choose either the head start, an intoxicating aromatherapy massage that focuses on face and arms, or the stress-busting face and scalp version, which includes a pressure point massage as well – the increased bloodflow will help your skin absorb whatever moisture comes its way.

Because my own skin is so dry (a situation not improved by a dose of African sun), I usually opt for the hydradermie facial. Once known as cathiodermie, this treatment uses high-frequency electrical currents to stimulate cell renewal and help my skin absorb the mask and moisturiser that follow more efficiently. What you end up with is squeaky-clean skin, which is then massaged, masked and moisturised until it feels soft and silky. Combine the facial with an aromatherapy body massage while you drift off to the distant sounds of animals readying themselves for another night's hunt. Africa does extraordinary things to your soul, but having Aroma Boma's therapists around to minister to your body's every need makes the whole experience even more rewarding.

Opulent
Abundant
Rich
Lavish
Luxuriant
Sumptuous

The very word, opulent, is a rich and round sound underlining its meaning. It is for the unashamedly self-indulgent. An opulent spa full of rich hangings, sumptuous fabrics, deep day beds and sensuous smells is a hedonist's heaven. It is where people go to spoil themselves, where they want to linger in warm pools, savour the rich oils and massages and lavish attention on themselves, their minds and their bodies. Opulent spas could almost have been invented for the work hard, play hard and spend hard generation, which demands and expects the best.

Opulent spas are big, not just in surface area but in spirit. Here is where you will find lavish treatment rooms with both indoor and outdoor bathing and massage areas, spacious and wildly glamorous steam rooms, swimming pools with underwater music and specialists from every corner of the earth. Opulence is magnificent privacy, when the spa and all it has to offer from wraps and anointings comes to you. Opulence is when two, not one, therapists join forces to soothe and stretch, pamper and cosset your body – when the magic and care of four hands provides far more then two ever could. Opulence is sensory extravagance.

The Assawan Spa, Burj Al Arab, Dubai.

The
Assawan
Spa

Dubai must surely be one of the wonders of the modern world – an entire universe conjured up out of the desert. Where once there was nothing but shifting sands now stands a city as modern as tomorrow. Somehow this future shift has been achieved without losing the essence of the Gulf, with its gold, spices and souks. The waters of Dubai's harbour swims with small dhows, which still sail to the furthest ports of Africa and Asia, plying their trade alongside the sleek super-yachts of sheiks, princes and captains of industry.

One of the state's most striking landmarks is the tallest hotel in the world – and, more than likely, the most costly to build. However you describe it, the Burj Al Arab is unmistakably the most opulent. Built in the shape of a sail as a tribute to Dubai's seafaring heritage, the Burj stands on its own man-made island a couple of hundred metres offshore at Jumeirah Beach. More than a mere building, the Burj is a structural tour de force that, within a few short years of its construction, has become just as much a statement of place as Paris's Eiffel Tower, Agra's Taj Mahal or New York's Empire State Building.

From the woven glass fibre of its sail to the soaring golden pillars of the reception area – not to mention the fountains that dance a ballet every 15 minutes in the world's tallest atrium – the Burj is more of an experience than a hotel, which is why non-residents are actually charged to come in and have a look. Whatever your vantage point, the view is extraordinary, from the eye-popping chandelier in the foyer to the glorious views of the Gulf from the restaurant perched at the top of the building – you reach it by express glass--fronted lift: not a trip for the faint-hearted. While the view from the summit may be the hotel's most spectacular, the journey to its seafood restaurant has to be the most bizarre – a virtual reality 'submarine' ride transports diners to the restaurant through an oceanscape of vividly-hued tropical fish and corals.

And then of course there is the spa, the Assawan, named after a local granite reputed to have healing powers, on the 18th floor of the hotel. Perhaps the spa's most striking feature is its extra-ordinary swimming pool, the ma'sama, which is built right up to the building's glass wall, giving swimmers the illusion that they are floating in the sky. With its plethora of colourful multi-patterned

mosaic columns and marble floors, the rest of the spa is no
less breathtaking.

As for treatments, the Assawan offers more than 50. Some
use all the modern expertise of the European beauty houses,
while others take their lead from the cultures of ancient Egypt,
China and India. Bathing rituals are among the most prominent
of Burj's offerings, and hydrotherapy is used in conjunction with
essential oils, marine extracts and even milk whey in a panoply
of sumptuous soakings – the latter is particularly efficacious for
soothing dry or sun-sore skin.

Essential oils based on the herbs and spices that have been
an integral part of Arabian and Asian cultures for centuries are
used in massages and wraps, and these aromatics are married
 with techniques gleaned from aromatherapy to energise the
body. Vetiver, parmarosa and geranium oils are particularly well
represented in the treatments, rosemary and pine are called
into play to help ease aching or tight muscles, while a special
anti-cellulite treatment uses a mixture of sea fennel, juniper and
lemon to smooth orange-peel skin.

There are also a number of treatments geared towards lymphatic
drainage and the fight against flabby, tired legs and thighs. One of
the most effective of these is the stimulating hip and thigh treatment
which begins with a seaweed and salt scrub – great for exfoliation –
and then moves onto a detoxifying massage with specially blended
oils, after which a warm marine algae gel is applied – the extracts
and minerals in this help fight blockages and water retention. And
the whole treatment is rounded off with a little reflexology and a
gentle lymphatic drainage massage around the eyes to remove
any puffiness.

Once you're all spa-ed out, take a trip into the desert, the very
essence of emptiness and silence – it's the best place in the world
to contemplate the vastness of the night skies. Have a massage,
then head for the stars.

Intricate detail, lavish inlay and precious
marbles underscore the sheer luxury of
the place.

Turnberry Isle

Not for nothing is Florida known as the sunshine state. Ever since the 1920s, its golden reputation has lured retirees escaping from cold northern climes, but these days it's fast becoming known as a year-round destination for all ages. Not only does the sun shine all year, the state also has two fantastic coastlines – the Atlantic and the Gulf of Mexico, any number of glittering islands and keys, and wonders both natural and man-made, from the Everglades to Disneyworld.

But although places like Disneyworld and Epcot are both creations of the American drive to innovate, to my mind the country's greatest invention of all is the all-purpose leisure resort– a place that offers virtually unlimited sporting activities, from sailing and volleyball to tennis and fishing, along with a host of restaurants, bars and shopping malls. Foremost among such resorts is Turnberry Isle, a very palace of leisure on Florida's Gold Coast. If it's not on offer at Turnberry, the chances are that it doesn't yet exist.

Apart from the two serious 18-hole championship golf courses designed by Robert Trent Jones Snr. – now de rigueur for any self-respecting US resort – Turnberry also has 19 tennis courts where former champion Fred Stolle keeps an eye on your play and a 117-slip marina for charter and deep-sea fishing yachts. There's an ocean club on the beach, complete with private cabanas, swimming pool and water sports centre. A resort so devoted to the physical would have been incomplete without a spa, and Turnberry's is a no-expense-spared number, with 10,000 square metres of wet rooms, dry rooms, special shower rooms, steam and inhalation rooms.

Housed in its own three-storey building adjacent to the main hotel entrance, the spa was designed by resort specialist Tag Galyean. He's used his skills to bring the Florida sunshine and tropical greenery indoors with walls of glass, plenty of running water and huge skylights that allow the light to flood through the space. The colours he's used are light and airy, apart from the aquas, blues and greens of the tile mosaics that bring to mind the waves of the nearby ocean.

Lavish though the building is, it's the excellence of the staff and the incredible range of treatments that are the spa's stars. The choice, influenced by the lore of India, Java, Thailand and Hawaii

Salts and mud, petals and potions – every ingredient is carefully chosen and effectively used.

is possibly one of the most extensive anywhere. The rituals the ancient Romans enjoyed in their public baths have been updated by technology to make the whole experience more comfortable, and muds and minerals from around the world have been investigated for their soothing and healing properties. Hi-tech gets a look-in, too, as the most up-to-date research from France and the United States has been incorporated into the products used in massages and facials. It's a veritable United Nations of treatments.

In an ideal world it would be wonderful to spend a month here and try the lot – back in real life, however, I would opt for the shea butter treatment. It's fantastic for older skins or for those who have had too much sun and wind out on those golf courses. It begins with a very gentle exfoliation, which is followed by a Vichy shower massage. While you lie on the massage table, seven shower heads are directed at various parts of your torso to warm and massage your muscles. Things get even better when your masseur begins to rub you with a very light oil at the same time as the water is gently played over your body. All those knotted muscles just fade away into nothingness. After you've dried yourself off, shea butter is applied all over – I swear I can almost hear my skin drinking it in.

While you're there, it would be a pity not to experience one of the specialised therapeutic baths as well. These are the spa's signature treatments, and are all based on natural essences and flowers – jasmine to reduce stress, orchid for relaxation, magnolia to recharge, milk to soften your skin and Dead Sea salt crystals to soothe aching muscles. If you want to get down and dirty, try one of the mud treatments. You can choose between a mud from Tuscany's Poretta Spa and another from the Dead Sea – the former is a great cleanser while the minerals in the latter are terrific for soothing sore muscles.

New treatments are being investigated constantly and incorporated into the already extensive menu. There's some exciting research into the herbal knowledge of Australia's aboriginal community, and some recent news from laboratories in Switzerland that are looking into anti-ageing solutions. From the looks of things, Turnberry is determined to keep its edge and remain in its current position as one of the world's top spas.

Sandy Lane, St James, Barbados.

Sandy Lane

With its grand houses, fabulous gardens and memorable beaches, Barbados definitely has the edge over the rest of the Caribbean when it comes to old-style glamour. It's been pulling in the glitterati for decades, from the Cunards in the 1930s to Mick Jagger and Joan Collins today, while reggae star Eddie Grant has a studio on the island, a magnet for today's rock royalty. But it's not all rock 'n' roll – Barbados stages its own opera and theatre festivals every year, and has a National Trust of its very own to look after all those historic houses. The mix of street smart with traditional elegance is a heady one that attracts thousands of visitors to the island each year, and some of the most sophisticated make a beeline for Sandy Lane each time.

For over 40 years now, the name Sandy Lane has been almost synonymous with Barbados. Although the island boasts a number of grand and luxurious hotels, this pink-and-cream edifice has always been considered the grandest and most luxurious of all. It's the kind of place where the rich and famous go to be with the rich and famous. If you're not famous, you'll just have to be rich if you want a taste of the Sandy Lane lifestyle, which begins with its location on the island's finest white-sand beach, St James. It offers everything you would expect from a top Caribbean resort: luxurious rooms with marble bathrooms, a great beach, loads of water sports, the ultimate in swimming pools, three dining areas, 27 holes of golf (soon to rise to 45) and the largest, most opulent spa on the island.

This almost circular building, with its rotunda and columns, takes its architectural inspiration from ancient Rome. A sweeping curved staircase takes guests into the spa proper, to changing and showering areas, steam rooms and saunas, as well as indoor and outdoor relaxation areas where you can doze in between treatments. The star of the show is an exquisite chakra therapy room, for meditation and relaxation while the Laconium steam room has an enormous amethyst crystal which brings with it it's calming and healing properties. The room has a heated marble plinth where you can meditate or simply relax, aided by the amethyst, which apparently helps to calm the weary traveller.

You won't be surprised to learn that the Sandy Lane spa offers a whole host of treatments, rituals, holistic therapies and wraps,

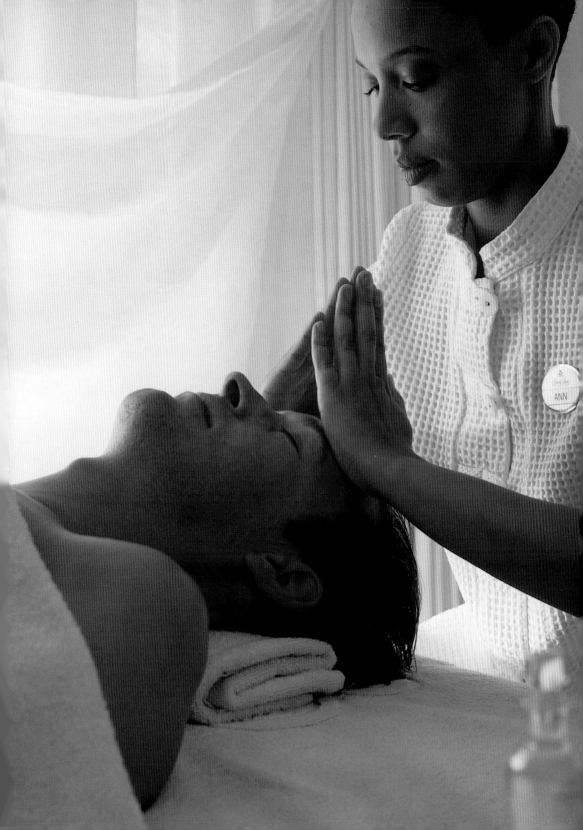

as well as a number of spa day programmes designed to tackle everything from a quick detox to some serious pampering. There's even a special pre-natal programme that features a gentle massage with muds, creams and calendula oil (a great weapon in the battle against stretch marks), an aromatherapy facial and a range of holistic foot and nail treatments. Pregnant or not, if you fancy finding an excuse to avoid the beach for a day you need look no further than a six-and-a-half-hour complete pampering package known as – what else? – the total indulgence. Book one and you're letting yourself in for a day-long session that takes care of it all, from a jet blitz to a hydrotherapy bath, rebalancing facial, hand and foot treatments and the Sandy Lane signature full body massage.

Don't forget to try one of the local Bajan treatments – which use native plants and herbs. India makes its presence felt, too, with a range of ayurvedic therapies. These include a special foot treatment, which works on stimulating the marma points – similar to acupuncture points – easing tension and improving the circulation. Like many ayurvedic treatments, it can be totally relaxing – or, if you're stressed out, quite the opposite, so approach with caution. If stress is a factor, an ayurvedic holistic total body treatment should help to redress your body-mind balance. The inward path begins with an infusion of herbs, which you sip while your feet are bathed and gently massaged. This is followed by an all-over marma massage, which includes the pressure points on the face, and ends with a head and scalp massage. Instant and near-total relaxation.

While the total body treatment is a great way to start a holiday, and would definitely be my choice if my feet were in order, somehow whenever I find myself near sand, sea and sun, my appendages really let me down. Uncared-for, tatty with chipped nail polish, they do nothing for my self-esteem, especially when I'm in a place where I want to go about barefoot or in sandals. That's why I always opt for the spa's holistic foot and nail treatment (exfoliation and a soothing massage with oils, followed by polish) before I can start to relax and enjoy the kind of toe-to-top treatment that has put – and kept – Sandy Lane firmly on the A-list of spa connoisseurs the world over.

Banyan Tree, Phuket, Thailand.

Banyan
Tree

Phuket has a reputation for being crowded and noisy, but once you move away from the beaches around Patong and Kara, the hubbub soon fades. A sleepy lagoon on the northwest of the island is home to five resorts, each completely different. The only things the resorts share is a passion for the environment, an inland waterway, an elephant camp and a great shopping centre – and one of the best spas on the planet – Banyan Tree Spa, Phuket.

In the heat of Thailand's tropics, a sense of space is vital. You need it for the air to circulate, for gardens to be lush and salas cool. No spa exhibits calm tropical opulence in quite the same way as the Banyan Tree – from the generous design of the open-sided pavilions and the luxurious abundance of the bougainvillaea-filled gardens to the numerous waterways that carry boats and guests through to the neighbouring lagoon. It's official – in the tropics, size matters.

Public areas are cathedrals to light, crafted in such a way that the rays of the sun are captured but its heat is deflected by open-sided rooms and the deployment of fountains and pools. Individual villas have their own garden, sundeck and open-air sunken bath; many have their own swimming pool or jacuzzi. Furnishings are simple but sumptuous: low tables made from teak, chaise lounges and sofas are upholstered in silk, huge brass pots filled with lotus blooms, bowls filled with mangosteen, rambutan and mango, and the pervasive scent of perfumed candles.

The spa itself is a sanctuary for the senses. A vast structure houses an infinity pool that seems to spill its waters out into the lush gardens, as well as treatment rooms and pavilions, a fitness centre, steam rooms, saunas and a beauty garden dedicated to hair and beauty treatments. The Tamarind Spa Restaurant is devoted to serving the healthiest food from Thailand, Japan and all points east, as well as juices of crushed carrot and mint, papaya and strawberry.

Many of the treatment areas are set in their own gardens, so that guests can choose whether to have them in the cool environs of the Thai sala or in the dappled sunlight under the shade of a frangipani tree. Sounds tempting, but the best is yet to come – wait until you find out about the therapies. A more mouth-watering selection would be tough to find. Asian traditions have provided the backbone of the treatment menu, fleshed out with a myriad of natural ingredients, from the local white mud, which has a cleansing effect, and traditional herbs and essences, to the fruits of the sea and the forest. Cleansing with rice and sandalwood is often followed by moisturising with yoghurt; cucumbers and honey are used in the traditional Thai facials while tamarind and oatmeal are used in combination to exfoliate and moisturise the skin.

Traditionalists will love the true Thai healer, featuring an ancient yoga massage and Thai herbal wrap, in which the therapist not only uses her palms, elbows and thumbs on the body's pressure points but often her whole body too, to stretch tired limbs and muscles. First-timers are offered a slightly less intimidating version of Thai massage in the special Asian blend therapy. In other treatments the rituals of Java and Bali mingle with Swedish know-how and Hawaiian therapies.

If you have never had a four-handed massage, this could well be the time and place to try one. Having two therapists working in synchrony on your body is one of the most relaxing experiences in the universe. With one therapist working on you, you have a fair idea of where the pressure is going to land next. With two therapists you have no idea and so you stop thinking about it, or even trying to prepare yourself for a bit of tension busting in a particularly painful spot. Within seconds your mind goes into neutral, within minutes you'll slip into a near-coma of relaxation – it's so wonderful that coming back to reality at the end of the session is a rude awakening, in more ways than one.

Those who take their pleasures seriously should opt for a full day of pampering in a place where even the manicure and pedicure takes a couple of hours, so much cosseting do they entail. The Banyan Day, all seven hours of it, includes a choice of body rub and wrap, a face and hand massage and then a full body massage. After which there is a spa cuisine lunch before embarking on a facial, manicure and pedicure to complete the day. But the greatest therapy of all is having the time and space to indulge your every desire, a dream Banyan Tree was built to fulfil.

Herbs and flowers, spices and poultices are all a part of ancient Thai traditions, which are used here in massages, wraps and scrubs.

Willow Stream Spa, The Fairmont Scottsdale Princess, Arizona, USA.

Willow
Stream
Spa

A rizona is a state of physical extremes – high mountain slopes plunge vertiginously into deep canyons and arid deserts are interspersed with welcome, cooling oases. Colours are vivid in the bright sunshine – rocks in deep shades of red and ochre are dramatically spliced with black – and at sunset the entire place looks as if it's on fire.

While many come to Arizona for the year-round sunshine that has turned the state into America's playground, the Fairmont Scottsdale Princess is one of the foremost resorts in the area, attracting many visitors in its own right. The hotel is sporting heaven. Some of the top names in world tennis flock here to play in its annual tournaments, and it offers seven floodlit tennis courts to mere mortals for the rest of the year. This is also cowboy country and, next to the hotel, you'll find Westworld. This 90-hectare horse park not only has 11 equestrian arenas, geared to all levels of experience, it also has its own polo ground and stabling for up to 500 horses. Perhaps more famously, the Scottsdale Princess also has what may well be two of the best championship golf courses in the world – the Desert Course and the Stadium Course, the latter famous for its 18th hole, which has sufficient space to accommodate up to 40,000 spectators.

As you might have gathered, the Fairmont Princess does everything on a grand scale and its spa, the Willow Stream, is no exception. I often think that spas are the golf widow's revenge. Although some women are happy whiling away their holidays on the greens, others need something apart from a number five iron to keep them amused. Nowadays, there's hardly a great golf course in the world that doesn't come with a fantastic spa attached, whether you're teeing off in North America or Southeast Asia.

As a direct response to its surroundings, the spa offers guests the inspire your senses desert spa package, which includes a three-hour private guided tour of the desert. You travel either by jeep or on foot to find the local flora and fauna used in spa treatments in their native habitats and, as you go, your guide will tell you about the area's history, its native people and the lives of the early settlers. The experience continues back at the spa with a two-hour havasupai body oasis – featuring exfoliation, massage and rehydration – that was inspired by the nearby Havasu Falls, a hidden oasis within the

Grand Canyon. An Arizona aromatherapy facial concludes the package – there's even a choice of aromatic ingredients, depending on whether you're after more energy, a release from stress or relaxation. It's a great way to see the area and experience what the spa has to offer, especially for first-timer visitors to the state.

Many treatments – particularly those geared towards soothing sun-damaged or extra-dry skin – involve the use of extracts of aloe vera, a cactus known for its cooling, moisturising properties. When you snap the plant's stem, the gel-like sap that oozes out can be applied straight to the skin. It feels much more luxurious, however, when it's turned into creams and lotions to be applied during soothing wraps, massage and facials. At this spa, they blend the aloe with pure algae and essential oils to help the skin absorb its healing properties that bit faster. There's also a sublime Anasazi aloe eucalyptus scrub, in which a mix of mineral salts and eucalyptus oil is applied all over your body, after which you are scrubbed with a loofah before being smoothed over with soothing aloe lotion.

And, of course, the spa offers special therapies for golfers. These include a Willow Stream exclusive, the golf performance treatment, a combination of massage, stretching and acupressure designed to improve flexibility and, thus, golfing performance, as well as to relieve golf-induced aches. Tempting as the range of treatments is, there's one you really shouldn't miss: the East-meets-West LaStone therapy. All four elements are brought into play – local basalt stones (earth) come from the river (water) and are heated (fire) and used in conjunction with specially blended oils of rose, basil, rosemary and sage to create a unique aroma (air) to help calm the mind and de-stress the body. All that and the desert, too – how much more natural magic could you want?

Polly Mar Beauty Spa

There are strong cultural and historic links between southern Spain and North Africa, and I'm reminded of them every time I visit the Costa del Sol, with its picturesque bays and coves, grand beaches and tiny whitewashed fishing villages. Over the past 50 years or so, some of these small villages – Marbella, Estepona and Puerto Banus – have been transformed into seriously glitzy towns that attract the rich and famous in droves.

One of the places they stay is Estepona's Kempinski Hotel, from whose glorious sub-tropical gardens you can see right across the straits to the place where North Africa rises from the sea. The design of the hotel, with its intricate plasterwork, tiled floors and domes, celebrates the links between the two continents in its mélange of Andalucian and Moorish styles. The vast edifice, resplendent with towers and verandas, appears to glow pink in the fierce Andalucian sunshine, the effect softened by the gardens full of palm trees and bougainvillaea. Three luxurious interlocking swimming pools provide the centrepiece of the gardens and, by wandering down a quiet pathway, you'll find the Polly Mar Beauty Spa.

The spa's exotic mix of therapies was devised by German spa queen, Polly Hillbrunner, who prides herself on her holistic approach to feeling good, calling into play the best nature has to offer. She relies on pure flower essences and the healing properties of seawater and marine plants. Carefully chosen fruits and vegetables are used in the spa's café to make juices and salads, and the same degree of consideration has been given to the materials and colours used in the décor.

You can feel your stress ebbing away the minute you enter this oasis of calm. Cool showers and warm baths form part of the large menu of treatments, which feature water-based therapies that range from authentic Finnish saunas to an Arabian rasul. Both underwater massage and hydroacupressure baths use warm seawater, with all its health-giving minerals, to enhance their therapeutic effects; while an invigorating, exfoliating scrub with sea salt is the ideal way to prepare the body for a Neptune shower-paradise. This specially designed treatment features warm aromatic oils that are massaged into the body by two masseurs under a shower of warm water, leaving you relaxed to the point of total inertia.

The pièce de résistance is the rasul de luxe, a recreation of the temptations of an Arabian hammam. The room alone is worth the trip: it's a jewel box of mosaic floors, tiled walls, fitted seats and hidden showers, its domed ceiling decked out in turquoise, cream and purple and studded with tiny star-like lights. Before entering this sybarite's paradise, the body is showered and massaged with a creamy lemon-scented concoction that softens and moisturises the skin. Then the hammam takes over and, as the door closes, warm steam begins to rise, the main lights are dimmed and the starry lights appear overhead. As you sit back and relax, the heat and steam work their magic on aching muscles and tired limbs. Once the mist has receded, the sound of fountains wakes you gently from your reverie and a gentle rain falls from hidden vents in the ceiling and walls to revive you. The revitalising finale is a fairly vigorous massage.

Other specialities include an Asian massage in which the energy flow of the body is rebalanced by a therapist concentrating on acupressure points and meridian lines. Polly Mar's face classic is a rigorous, vigorous cleansing and peeling facial that incorporates a massage of the face, neck and décolleté. Perhaps unsurprisingly in a part of the world devoted to sea, sand and surf, there are a number of treatments dedicated to after-sun (and wind) care. All the products for these soothing treatments – face cool and body cool – use natural active extracts from aloe vera, tea tree and jojoba, all plants known for their healing properties.

Some of the most popular therapies, however, combat cellulite and are designed to reduce the number and size of fat cells. The treatment for the latter is the renowned Polly's sauna wrap cure original, at its most efficacious in a course of six. The wrap involves special herbal extracts and oils being bandaged onto the body and allowed to permeate in the hothouse atmosphere of a sauna, a period to allow the body to cool off, then a warm shower, after which the wrap is removed and a concluding massage is given.

Tourists may well come to the Costa del Sol for the ritzy glamour of Marbella or the serene splendour of the great Moorish cities of southern Spain – Granada, Seville and Cordoba – but the Polly Mar Beauty Spa provides the ideal place to retire from the fray and recharge your batteries in exotic, pampered seclusion.

175 Polly Mar Beauty Spa, Kempinski Resort Hotel, Estepona, Spain.

Six Senses Spa, Soneva Gilli, Lankafushi Island, Maldives.

Six Senses Spa

I n a country consisting completely of islands, it is difficult to find one more beautiful than another. All the islands in the Maldives have the prerequisite perfect soft, white sandy beaches; clear, warm, inviting turquoise seas; and wonderfully luxurious hotels.

Lankanfushi Island on the Hudhuveli lagoon, part of the Malé Atoll, is no exception. However, the thing that makes the island's resort, Soneva Gili, one of the largest in the Maldives, unique is that it is set mainly on water. All the villas, suites and residences perch over the lagoon on stilts, and many of their sundecks give the impression that they're floating off to sea. The resort is surrounded by a coral reef, which means you hardly need to don a snorkelling mask to spot the jewel-bright creatures swimming below your feet. Naturally, no self-respecting island resort would be without its own fully equipped diving school, catering for beginners as well as aficionados, and, again, Soneva Gili is no exception.

I'm not sure about the whole thing, however. Why, I ask myself, move at all if you can see glorious fish while reclining on the deck of your own villa? Why interrupt the pursuit of pleasure with any unnecessary activity when every luxury can be brought directly to you? Why even bother going to the restaurant when a floating kitchen can come right to your door? Why, indeed, head for the spa if it can come to you? Want a massage? You can have it on your roof terrace or deck. Want a massage à deux with your beloved, either under the stars or to an aural backdrop of waves crashing on the shore – or both? No problem, the Six Senses Spa will make it all happen for you. The soothe the senses treatment combines herbal infusions, soft, warm towels and aromatherapy oils. Or go for broke and choose an indulge the senses package and have not one, but two, therapists work on your body (and his) with a special Aphrodite mix of oils (don't ask) to set the mood before retiring to leave you both to enjoy a bottle of champagne afterwards.

I suppose, after a day or two, you may feel like moving – a little bit. To make things that extra bit easier, bridges connect all the villas to the main resort and spa. The privileged few, those staying in the seven luxurious Robinson Crusoe residences, which can only be reached by water, will need to get there in their own rowing boat (complete with person to row), moored at their private jetty. The reception area and restaurant, as well as the dive centre and

179 Six Senses Spa, Soneva Gilli Resort, Lankafushi Island, Maldives

tennis courts are based on land, but all the other facilities, from the bar to the spa, are a bridge away. It's an extraordinary sensation, as if you're walking on water wherever you go. One's thing for sure – everyone staying at Soneva Gili gets to enjoy that immense sense of relaxation that comes from being surrounded by gently lapping waves.

To get the most from each treatment, guests are advised to arrive early enough to spend time in the sauna or steam room so that both muscles and mind are relaxed before the sessions begin. Should you want the works, I'd recommend the sixth sense treatment – two hours of complete, unadulterated pampering. After a full body exfoliation, followed by a body mask wrap, which seals in the heat and helps detox the body, the face is cleansed, massaged, refreshed and moisturised. Once the mask is removed, it's time for the full body massage, which uses specially selected oils. Or perhaps you would prefer the feast the senses treatment, a Thai-style massage that concentrates on your back, followed by reflexology and a leg massage. It's a great reviver. Another of the treatments for couples – known, appropriately enough, as Adam and Eve – involves dual facials, head massages, manicures and pedicures and are incredibly popular with honeymooners. Beach lovers should try the sense Maldives massage, which uses refined sand and seawater to exfoliate any rough patches. Best of all, it actually takes place on the beach.

Whatever you do though, don't miss the cocoon treatment. A mixture of seaweed and mud is smoothed over your body before you are tightly wrapped, first in a sort of clingfilm, then in blankets and towels. The warmth this generates not only rids the body of excess fluids and toxins, but also aids the rehydrating effect of the mud. A follow-up massage of moisturising body oils is indescribably luxurious, and leaves your skin feeling incredibly smooth.

When you finally feel ready for a little activity, consider a swimming lesson. Whether you usually swim like a stone, or just want to tune up your award-winning butterfly, there's no better place to learn than in the calm, warm waters of this Maldivian lagoon. There's an instructor on staff, the water is warm and the sea translucent. It just couldn't be easier.

Givenchy Spa, Le Saint Géran, Mauritius.

Givenchy Spa

With its mix of French, English, Indian and Chinese settlers, Mauritius has always been the most cosmopolitan of islands. These days, of course, it's become even more diverse as visitors from Southeast Asia, the USA, Europe and Australia flock to its shores in search of the ultimate island paradise. This is the place where British honeymooners rub shoulders with bankers from Frankfurt, where Italian designers hang out with wine growers from Australia's Barossa Valley, and where South African farmers unfold their beach towels next to those belonging to video kings from Los Angeles. This international melting pot enjoys the best of all worlds – so it's not surprising to learn that its glitziest spa is French.

There are few spas in the world that can match the elegant splendour of Mauritius's Givenchy spa. To begin with, it's based at the grandest hotel on the island, Le Saint Géran. And, from its setting, which looks out onto the lagoon on one side and lush tropical gardens on the other, to its extensive treatment list, this is a spa that simply oozes luxury. The first thing you notice about it is its large infinity pool, which makes swimmers feel as if they are heading straight out to the ocean. Dotted around the pool, overlooking the ocean and miles of white sands, are relaxation areas where the worn-out await their treatments and the already-pampered purr in the sun. Several treatment rooms, some dedicated to hydrotherapy, lead off from the pool area, as does a fitness centre devised by London's personal training guru, Matt Roberts, and an offshoot of Paris's most fashionable hairdressing salon, Jean Marc Maniatis.

The big names don't stop at the poolside. The grounds are home to a golf academy that was set up by David Ledbetter – the man who changed the Faldo swing, and the tennis club is affiliated to the Peter Burwash Institute – one of the foremost tennis coaching schools in the world. Not to be outdone, the hotel houses one of the world-renowned Alain Ducasse restaurants – Spoon des Iles.

It comes as no surprise, then, to find that the spa is run by Givenchy, one of the top names in the beauty world. So elite are the Givenchy spas that there are only a handful of them scattered around the globe. This one combines the very best of Parisian chic with the laid-back glamour of the island itself – a heady blend

indeed. Every single treatment has been devised or reformulated by Givenchy to incorporate its own range of essences, creams and lotions. Even the hot stone massage has been adapted to the house philosophy: volcanic stones taken from the river beds of the American West are used in combination with a specially formulated Givenchy oil to help clients detox and relax. Of course, being French, they refer to the treatment as the canyon love stone therapy. Massages include the sportif, which is particularly good for muscles and joints aching after a hard round of tennis or several games of golf; a lymphatic drainage that helps the body rid itself of toxins, which make the circulation sluggish and the skin dull; and a whole range of Swedish, aromatherapy and relaxing massages. If I had to pick one, I'd be tempted by the exceptional four-handed massage with ylang-ylang oil. The flower grows throughout Mauritius and has a heady fragrance that could only have been born of the heat and abundance of a tropical island, while the sheer luxury of having two people focus on your body at the same time is the ultimate sensual experience.

Massages notwithstanding, it's the facials for which the French are best known, and at Le Saint Géran they approach them with a rigorous desire to improve not just the skin but also the underlying muscles, thus preventing sagging around the jawline. Beauty therapists trained in Paris cleanse skin like zealots – no crevice is left unscoured, no impurity left to fester, nor a single stray hair allowed to spoil the line of a brow. Once the hard work is over, the face is massaged and masqued. As a quintessentially French company, Givenchy has a whole menu of facials. Some of these are merely relaxing, while others drain away puffiness or concentrate on lifting and tightening. I'd advise you to go for a consultation beforehand – the therapist will examine your skin closely before suggesting the best course of treatment. The one I always choose is a rejuvenating and revitalising treatment that uses incredibly rich ingredients to work miracles by nourishing older, drier skins.

It must be something about the magic of Mauritius that makes every element of Le Saint Géran appear so effortless, from the perfectly raked beaches to the efficient elegance of the spa. Both require great effort but you, as a guest, are never aware of it – all you have to do is lie back and enjoy the result.

Serene

Calm
Composed
Tranquil
Peaceful
Restful

In an over-stressed world everybody is searching for calm, tranquillity and peace of mind, for that serene state of being where life is clear and untroubled. A state we all aspire to and in the pursuit of which we seek out resorts, spas and retreats. We hope that a soothed and pampered body may help induce a calm and tranquil mind.

Serenity is what we hope for when we take a walk on the seashore, a ramble through the countryside or a pause in a garden. We look outward for an inner calm, and it is this need which propels us towards spas where in relaxed and tranquil surroundings we hope to find that inner peace.

For in such artificially evoked environments we seek simplicity and serenity. In order to do this the range of help available is awe-inspiring — from ancient philosophies and therapies through to state of the art techniques and equipment, from a myriad of exercise disciplines to art classes, and from beauty treatments to life management courses. They will even teach us to breathe again — truly, properly and deeply.

Chiva-Som, Hua Hin, Thailand.

Chiva-Som

Chiva-Som is the resort of choice for Thailand's royal family. Every summer they decamp from the heat and humidity of Bangkok and head south to the Gulf of Siam to enjoy its balmy sea breezes and the long, curved golden beach. Well-heeled Thais and the occasional farang (foreign) tourist soon followed, but it was only fairly recently that it became the location for Asia's first purpose-built health resort, Chiva-Som.

The first purpose-built spa in Thailand still leads the field in traditional therapies combined with modern research.

The brainchild of a former deputy prime minister, the resort leaves nothing to chance, from the flowers and trees planted in the gardens to the teak and marble used in the pavilions and villas. Silks from northern Thailand create a textural contrast to the lacquerware and basketwork from other parts of the country, and cool cottons and hand-glazed ceramics are used throughout. Natural light pours in through large windows to enhance the materials within and the views of beach and sea without.

The spa lies at the centre of the resort and every guest begins with a health and wellness consultation, after which the vast array of treatments and therapies is at their disposal. The massage pavilion, for instance, has special rooms for all types of massage, including traditional Thai, which takes place on a floor mattress with the therapist using his or her body to work and stretch the prostrate guest for the most invigorating rub imaginable. A bathing pavilion incorporates an exercise pool, massage waterfalls and a Kneipp therapy footbath, where hot and cold water alternate to boost circulation. Outside, on the beach's sandy fringes, there's a large swimming pool. Water is the key to Chiva-Som's treatments, and the elegant glass and marble hydrotherapy suite, with its swirling massage baths and therapeutic showers, has a whole range of treatments devoted to improving circulation, toning muscles and reducing cellulite. The pavilion is also home to one of the largest and most glamorous flotation pools in southeast Asia.

Therapies deal with everything from tired muscles to aching legs: wraps and exfoliations rub shoulders with self-heating mud treatments, loofah scrubs and oriental foot massages. There's complementary medical therapies on offer, too – these include iridology and hypnotherapy alongside the newer dulayaphap-bumbud, an alternative acupuncture that de-clogs blocked energies

Thai massage unblocks energies as every bit of the body is stretched and kneaded. Known by many as the yoga massage, it is the great energiser.

and is used to treat all types of ailments, from asthma to arthritis.

The active are well catered for, with classes that range from body sculpting to Thai boxing; but an early-morning tai chi class in the open air pavilion by the beach is one of Chiva-Som's chief delights. No matter how late I went to bed the previous night, this morning class soon became a must, as much for the privilege of watching the sun rise in such a stunning setting as for the exercise itself. And, while tai chi appears gentle and restrained to the casual onlooker, to the participant it can feel extremely strenuous. A Chinese martial art, it relies on slow, sustained movements coupled with great concentration and slow, deep breathing to achieve a balance between mind and body. It also stretches the limbs, assists balance and improves the circulation, not to mention its capacity to invigorate – after an hour's class one feels incredibly energised.

Food is, of course, vital to well-being and although Thailand has one of the world's great cuisines, with all its high-fat coconut cream and peanut oil, it's not necessarily as healthy as you might think. The chefs at Chiva-Som have devised ways of keeping the tastes and textures of traditional Thai food by using stock and unsweetened fruit purées while losing much of the fat content. As much of the food as possible is sourced locally, and most vegetables and herbs are grown in the resort's own gardens. Along with organising cookery demonstrations, the chefs are usually happy to take visitors on a guided tour of the kitchen gardens to show them the range of produce grown there.

In spite of such a wealth of activities and therapies, the real joy of Chiva-Som is its sense of tranquillity. The guest pavilions are spacious and so private that one might never come into contact with other guests. The gardens are large and designed so that a number of hidden areas and quiet arbours provide peace and respite. Then there's the beach – miles of silvery pale sand washed by the gentle waters of the Gulf of Siam. See it at dawn with the pale rose of a rising sun adding a blush to the breaking waves or take a stroll in the moonlight under a sky full of stars embedded in stillness – by day or by night, Chiva-Som is the absolute embodiment of serenity.

Canyon Ranch Spa and Health Resort, Tucson, Arizona, USA.

Canyon
Ranch

Arizona, with its wide-open spaces, vast desert and extraordinary rock formations that reach their apogee in the Grand Canyon and Monument Valley, lies at the heart of the great American southwest. Once home to some 21 nations of Native Americans, the state is rich in culture and traditions. A place of fiery red rocks, great mountain ranges and the Sonoran Desert, Arizona also claims to be one of the most naturally spiritual places in the United States. This is due to a number of natural energy vortices – places, many believe where physical and spiritual energy, a sort of mysterious electromagnetic field, is released from the earth. As a consequence, a vast number of healers, therapists and new age practitioners have been drawn here and this is possibly where you will find some of the best in America. It also has a near-perfect climate – sunny and dry with no humidity – which has become a magnet for some spectacular spas and health resorts.

Canyon Ranch is one such place. A former working ranch, it is now a serious spa resort. Tucked away on a 15-hectare estate, it offers treatments that can range in duration from one hour to several days, while its life enhancement centre runs week-long programmes throughout the year. These range from stress management courses to those offering advice on successful ageing, exploring your sexuality and avoiding heart disease. Each guest, after an initial consultation, is assigned their own programme co-ordinator, with whom they discuss what they hope to achieve from their visit – weight loss, inch loss, sleep enhancement or relaxation are among the specific goals you can tackle. Together, you set about trying to achieve these aims. Along the way you can consult with behavioural therapists, clinical psychologists, nutritionists, chiropractors, physiotherapists, acupuncturists, ayurvedic specialists and Chinese herbalists, not to mention masseurs, beauticians and physical instructors. Canyon Ranch is nothing if not serious about your well-being.

Physical health is all-important, and nine gyms and three swimming pools are dedicated to improving the physique and fitness of guests. There are also more than 50 classes and lectures each day, whose topics include yoga, breathing and meditation. What's more, the resort has its own meditation dome, a place of amazing peace and calm.

There's also a wide range of treatments on the spa menu. In particular, there are many forms of massage, from Thai through to a special Canyon Ranch stone massage, in which warm basalt stones are used to help release tensions and soothe muscles, and lymphatic massage for those with water retention problems. There is also a number of alternative treatments, based on ayurvedic, reiki and cranio-sacral therapies. There's a brilliant treatment called euphoria – so named because that's exactly the sensation the therapists hope to induce. First, you're wrapped in warm blankets, herb-infused towels cover your face and a scalp massage perfumed with rose geranium oil takes place. Afterwards once you have reached the critical relaxation zone, a full body mask is applied. When it has wrought its miracles, you are left to soak in a warm tub to which grapefruit oil has been added. The whole thing finishes with a massage – euphoria indeed.

Anyone who's spent too much time in the bright Arizona sunshine should try the skin treatment called aloe cooler. A soothing aloe vera gel is first applied, followed by rosehip and aloe cream for extra rehydration. Finally you are enveloped in a delicate mist of lavender oil. For those with sensitive or sun-dried skin, there's the mango sugar glo – a great exfoliant made up of a mix of fructose, beta-carotene and jojoba extracts, followed by a body wash and an application of moisturiser.

But wouldn't you know it, the one treatment I long to try is only available to men. Rejuvenating waters (to be haajidaah) take their name and idea from traditional Native American sweat lodges – it begins with a hydrotherapy treatment, then a steam, and finishes with a massage that uses stones and hot and cold towels to really unkink your muscles and get those toxins sweating out of your pores.

Never mind there is always the warm, wonderful climate and the relentless pampering you get at Canyon Ranch not to mention the spectacular scenery, to make up for my lack of a Y chromosome.

Meditation, yoga and tai chi classes are just a few of the de-stressing tools offered at the resort alongside desert hikes and total relaxation.

Willow Stream Spa, The Fairmont Banff Springs, Alberta, Canada.

Willow
Stream
Spa

There's only one word to describe the Canadian Rockies – awesome. To see them at their most magnificent, take a trip to the province of Alberta, where you'll see range upon range of snow-capped peaks, interspersed with huge forests, crystal-clear lakes and vast icefields.

All this means that no spa can have a more dramatic setting than Willow Stream, the spa at The Fairmont Banff Springs, deep in the stony heart of the Rockies. Great mountain peaks overlook the valley, the location for the hotel itself, a huge Victorian Gothic edifice. Its massive granite presence seem to brood over the area during the day, while at night, with lights twinkling from every window, it's transformed, as if by magic, into a fairytale castle.

The hotel was built in 1888 by the visionary entrepreneur of the Canadian Pacific Railway, William Cornelius van Horne. He not only constructed one of the world's great train lines, he also built some of the world's great railway hotels – and this was the first of them. His dream was to bring the comforts of civilisation to the heart of the Rockies, and to entice travellers to such a remote place he promised: "You shall see mighty rivers, vast forests, boundless plains, stupendous mountains and wonders innumerable; and you shall see all in comfort, nay, in luxury". The man did not exaggerate.

Not only is the scenery spectacular and the hotel the epitome of comfort, the original spa offered Turkish and Russian baths, private sulphur baths, Swedish massage and a freshwater pool. The spa was virtually abandoned during the early part of the last century, until seven years ago. The new spa was designed to conform to our contemporary desires for a more global approach to pampering – among the innovations were Finnish saunas, Hungarian thermal mineral baths, shiatsu from Japan, reflexology and acupuncture from China, thalassotherapy treatments from France.

As you might expect from a place that offers such a vast menu of treatments, the spa is huge – some 3,500 square metres of space has been turned over to create 25 treatment rooms, a large indoor heated saltwater swimming pool, an outdoor heated pool, an indoor Hungarian therapeutic spa mineral pool, an outdoor whirlpool and three cascading waterfall massage pools (all at different temperatures and pressures). Water definitely plays a huge part in these treatments – of which there are more than 60 in total.

209 Willow Stream Spa, The Fairmont Banff Springs, Alberta, Canada

Make sure you try the signature pine herbal bath, a great relaxer for those who come to Banff to hike, play golf or ski. The place is surrounded by pine forests and on a crisp, clear day the trees perfume the entire area, so it feels thoroughly appropriate to bathe in the stuff. Other mineral and herbal baths include a therapeutic Hungarian mineral bath, a great aid to detoxification, and a traditional German kur bath, whose aromatic wildflower oils help to ease aching muscles. Afterwards, indulge in any one of the spa's massages – there's relaxation, shiatsu, aromatherapy, reflexology or even a deep-tissue therapeutic version. All in all, it's a great way to spend an hour or so.

There are also scrubs with salts and pumice stones, body brushing, aromatic wraps and Kur treatments. Enjoy an application of mineral-rich spirulina (an aquatic plant) gel. Its botanical and mineral extracts are brilliant at re-hydrating your body. The spirulina mixture is applied all over your body and you're wrapped in cellophane to sweat out the impurities. The added benefit is that the heat generated is fantastic at dealing with aching limbs. I love this treatment, not only for the effect it has on my skin, but also because it has a very therapeutic effect on any aches and pains I might be suffering. The greyish-brown gloop might look unappetising, but just think of what the trace minerals are doing for your skin. Once it's all been scrubbed off, you finish off with a relaxing bath. It's a wonderful antidote to a hard day's skiing (there are some fantastic slopes within 20 minutes of the hotel).

If you can't face it after a day on the piste, take a dip in the hotel's heated indoor pool before taking the plunge for real and heading outside to the even-warmer outdoor pool, where you can enjoy a panorama of snowy peaks as you swim. While your body is cocooned in the warm water, your head is cleared by the startlingly pure, ice-cold air. When you can bear the contrast no longer, make a beeline for the cascading showers and pools indoors, where all your aching joints will be massaged until they are pain-free. Just be warned – the last shower and pool are so cold that they're only for the brave.

The Rockies at their most magnificent – great for walking in during summer, magnificent for skiing down in the winter.

The Aman Spa, Amanpuri, Pansea Beach, Phuket, Thailand.

Aman Spa

Phuket is Thailand's largest island and, for that reason, it's the most developed, with resorts, marinas, markets and hotels. But it's not difficult to find peace and calm in the place; simply head for the west coast where, high on a headland overlooking the Andaman Sea, the entrance to another world awaits. Here, in the shelter of a lush coconut grove, you'll find 40 of the most exquisite pavilions you will ever know, scattered almost nonchalantly towards the white sands of the beach. You have reached Amanpuri.

A passion for privacy has been one of the hallmarks of the Aman resorts – and this is where it all started on a headland overlooking the Andaman Sea. It is also the site of the first Aman spa.

Some time ago, a new species of traveller was identified on this planet – the Amanjunkie. A particular group of people who spend their holidays travelling around to all the Aman resorts – breathtakingly exquisite hotels, most of which are sited in far-flung places. The creator of the Aman phenomenon, Adrian Zecha, together with American architect Ed Tuttle, has elevated forever our expectations of what a world-class hotel should be. And no matter how many fledgling establishments have tried to copy the extraordinary elements of Aman – whether it be the soaring reception areas, infinity pools, suites with luxurious furnishings and private splash pools, well-stocked libraries and more – none have quite managed to emulate Aman's essence. This essence lies both in the detail and in the successful relationship between the buildings of each resort and their surroundings. Amanpuri, for example, took as its inspiration the temples of Ayutthaya – the old capital of Thailand – with their great soaring roofs and sense of space.

It is no wonder that the Sanskrit word amanpuri means 'place of peace'. So peaceful are the pavilions, each with its own outdoor sala (private sundeck and dining terrace), that many guests rarely venture out of them, except for the occasional foray to the beach just below the hotel or to the navy blue-tiled infinity pool for a gentle swim. Now, however, there is another reason to venture forth – a visit to the resort's spa – the first in the Aman group, which opened at the end of 2001. Here, overlooking the sea from the shelter of the coconut plantation, are six treatment pavilions, sauna, steam room and two outdoor salas designed specifically for yoga, meditation and a host of treatments and therapies.

As well as a number of specific spa programmes, which can last anything from three hours to five days, the spa has a multitude of

especially devised wraps, scrubs, baths and massage, all of which use the spa's own potions and lotions. These contain such nutritious-sounding ingredients that you find yourself wondering whether to eat them rather than have them applied to your face or body.

Take, for instance, the natural hair and scalp treatment, a mix of avocado and coconut milk that is massaged into the hair and scalp for 20 minutes. Not only is the smell sensational, the condition of your hair afterwards is even more so. And then there's the fruit facial – a combination of watermelon, banana, cucumber, herbs and natural yoghurt. The spa even gives you the recipe so that you can prepare it at home later on. Two treatments, one pre-sun and one after-sun, not only have great natural ingredients but also have a wonderful effect on the skin. The pre-sun treatment, which is a gentle exfoliation and massage of coconut, jasmine and rice, leaves your skin silky-smooth, while the after-sun treatment containing aloe vera, cucumber and banana, soothes and cools any redness or soreness.

Massages include Thai and Swedish as well as a healing version, which balances the chakras ruling our energy points; wraps include the special Thai din sor porng – a white mud traditionally used to cool and moisturise the skin – and the sweet-scented lavender clay wrap, which also contains sandalwood. There's the traveller's reviver, which helps fight jet-lag and, if your body clock is still awry, you can enjoy the sweet dreams treatment in the privacy of your own pavilion after dinner. Follow that with some relaxing camomile tea and you're sure to have a blissful night.

Finally, there's my choice, the soul to sole, where the two most stressed-out parts of my body are kneaded and soothed as I lie, listening to the breeze and the waves, in one of the treatment pavilions. First my back, neck and shoulders are massaged and manipulated to ease any tensions that might have built up and improve my circulation. As my blood starts to flow in that direction, the therapist turns her attention to my feet and delivers a vigorous massage. This is my idea of heaven. The only way it could get any better would be if I were to set sail across the Andaman Sea aboard one of the resort's 20 beautiful cruisers at sunset. It occurs to me that if I did, I, too, might end up an Amanjunkie.

The Spa Village, Pangkor Laut Resort, Malaysia.

Pangkor Laut Resort

The northwest coast of Malaysia is lined with forests and fringed with tiny fishing villages. Offshore lie a few islands, most of them no more than specks on the map. One of these is the private island of Pangkor Laut, a tiny dot of emerald floating in the brilliant blue waters of the Straits of Malacca, a short boat ride away from the mainland. On its shores, strung together by a series of beaches, are a number of perfect bays. One of these, Emerald Bay, surrounded by rainforest, is home to the most beautiful beach on the island. Another is home to a string of seafront villas, exquisite traditional Malaysian buildings with huge private decks. Guests have a choice of accommodation that includes water bungalows, exquisite cottages dotted on the hillside or grand villas called Estates with their own swimming pools. (Pavarotti chose a hillside suite, while Joan Collins preferred a beach front Estate for her latest honeymoon). Wonderful though both bays are, my personal favourite is the enticing Spa Village Bay.

The Spa Village, overlooking the straits, has a 50-metre lap pool that runs parallel to the beach, and a string of spa bungalows on stilts over the sea. Upon request, you can enjoy all your treatments in total privacy, either in the cool of the large bedrooms or on a private deck. But most treatments take place in one of eight beautifully simple pavilions, all built with local materials and adorned with traditional furniture.

All the treatments are based on the teachings and therapies of the four cultures that have influenced the region – Malaysian, Thai, Chinese and Indian. Ayurvedic specialists have been flown over from India to advise on treatments, while doctors of Chinese medicine are also available for consultation – each in their own specially decorated pavilions. The three open-air Thai pavilions specialise in massages and reflexology. The signature body treatments include a traditional herbal massage in which pouches of steamed lime leaves and lemongrass are pressed along the body's meridians to unblock trapped energies. The campur campur (which in Malay means a blending of varieties) massage combines the deep strokes of traditional Malaysian massage with the stretching of the Thai version to leave you feeling relaxed, yet surprisingly energised.

Begin your treatments in the bath-houses with the Chinese foot pounding, which relaxes you from the toes upwards and helps to get

The Spa Village – a whole area devoted to well-being on the tiny island of Pangkor Laut – has its own villas, restaurant, pool, treatment pavilions and bath house.

the circulation moving. You're then escorted to the cool, refreshing waters and showers of the Malay bathing pool before being led to the warmer water of the Japanese bathing area. Just before you get completely waterlogged, you're taken to a scrub room to indulge in a gentle, but thorough, Shanghai scrub, a top-to-toe lathering and loofah-ing. Squeaky-clean, you are led to your treatment room and the therapy of your choice (unless, of course, you choose to make a detour to the wrap room to revel in a Chinese herbal wrap that uses herbs to eliminate toxins and soften skins). There's a detoxifying spirulina version, too, which contains seaweed to help the job along; but then again, the local papaya enzyme wrap shouldn't be missed.

A session of tui na an mo, often known as tuina, comes highly recommended, Tuina is part of the repertoire of traditional Chinese medicine, as much a part of any healing process as acupuncture and herbalism. It is little known in the West, due to the years of study each practitioner must undergo. The massage is an unusual fusion of squeezing, pummelling and more conventional strokes which can feel quite painful at times. You know that it's doing you good, though, because you'll soon feel the blood coursing around your body as blockages are released. Afterwards, you feel supremely relaxed yet raring to go. There are quite a few Chinese therapies offered here, including a quan shen jin yu or herbal bath that harmonises the body's yin and yang, and the ancient practice of cupping. Here, heated glass cups are applied to your back to lower your temperature and release any trapped gases. If you're planning a session, I'd recommend you leave it until your last day as it leaves red marks on the body for a few days.

Otherwise, you can always do what I enjoy best. Once the massage is over, make a beeline for one of the three nap pavilions on the sand, where you can unwind by lying on deep cushions. The therapist pulls white muslin curtains around you for privacy and leaves you to nod off to the gentle rhythmic hiss of the waves. Bliss.

The Aveda Concept Spa

O f all the islands in the Caribbean, Jamaica alone defies categorisation. Sure, it's beautiful, with palm-strewn beaches and smart hotels aplenty, but it's not just a tourist destination. Glamorous, yet edgy, grand estates stand side by side with shanty towns, the golden beaches fringe a dense tropical interior. Wordsmiths such as Noel Coward and Ian Fleming chose the island as their second home, but it is its music that really put Jamaica on the world map. It's here that reggae was born, and you can't find a place on the island that doesn't echo to its throbbing beat.

In more ways than one, Strawberry Hill has the coolest setting in the Caribbean, right in the heart of Jamaica's Blue Mountains. The 12 cottages and suites have huge rooms: all white walls, wooden fretwork screens, enormous mahogany four-poster beds, ceiling fans and grand verandas packed with huge rattan chairs and hammocks where you can enjoy the heady mix of warm sunshine and cool mountain air. The effect is magical. In the early morning a true blue haze hovers over the mountain-tops, while in the evening the same peaks glow pink and gold in the sunset. The infinity-edged pool on the terrace of the main complex has glorious views over the trees to the rooftops of Irishtown beneath, beyond to Kingston, the capital, more than 1,000 metres below, and on to the great glittering turquoise expanse of the Caribbean.

Tranquillity surrounds you. But in the early evening, if you sit out on a veranda and strain your ears just a little, you can hear the sounds of a reggae beat filtering through from some local rum shop a few miles away. That's the moment you know you could not be anywhere else on earth but Jamaica. Savour it with a rum punch of your own – you can always walk off the effects the next morning with a hike to a coffee plantation (this is the place they grow the world's most expensive coffee) or, better still, take yourself off to the spa for a brisk morning-after massage, wrap or scrub.

The Aveda Concept Spa is housed in a separate villa, where large polished-wood treatment rooms open onto verandas, allowing cool breezes and the buzz of the humming birds to waft around you. On arrival, you'll be offered a sensory journey, in which you are presented with a number of oils and essences to choose from in order to create your own aroma identity. This essence, which is

often a mixture of two or three individual aromas, is then blended and used in all your treatments. All the essences and, consequently, all the therapies are based on natural flower and plant ingredients – among them sandalwood, ginger, ylang-ylang, vetiver and rose, to name but a few. You are encouraged to take as much time as you like on this sensory discovery, which is just as well, as each scent seems better than the one before. Not only do you keep changing your mind, you also keep going back for another sniff of something you might have dismissed first time round. But the therapists are patient and, somewhere along the way, you drift into Caribbean time, a pace where there is never a rush and nothing is ever a problem.

Once you've finally pinpointed your aroma identity, treatments can begin in earnest. The spa offers several types of massage, from the relaxing to the therapeutic, with a little shiatsu along the way. The body elixirs are remoisturising and rehydrating treatments that work miracles on dry, chafed skins or bodies that have had a little too much exposure to the sun and sea air. Special self-renewal face and body treatments are signature Aveda therapies. Treat yourself to a two-hour session: its facial incorporates massages for feet, neck and hands – any frown lines you came with should disappear almost instantly. The body session begins with exfoliation and ends with a serious massage that focuses extra attention on the more stressed-out bits of your neck, shoulders and upper back. The good bit for those with a phobia about full-on massage is that the pressure is directed by you.

The thing I look forward to most, though, each time I arrive at Strawberry Hill is special not just because of the treatment itself, but also because of its setting. I'm talking about the state-of-the-art pedicure, in which your feet are soaked and scraped, massaged and moisturised before the polish is applied. My preferred location? Out on the main terrace in the early evening, where I lie back and listen to the song of the tree frogs, backed by the distant dub reggae, as I wait for the stars to come out and the moment when I realise that, once again, I have fallen under Jamaica's spell.

The Over Water Spa

M ost visitors to the Maldives, that extraordinary archipelago of more than 1,000 islands in the Indian Ocean, expect to spend their time on just one island. Naturally, there might be time for an occasional sightseeing foray, a visit to a typical Maldivian village or a day trip to one of the smaller, more secluded islands, where picnic basket and parasol can be deployed to maximum effect. But most visitors are not inclined to budge from the luxury of their resorts. Guests at the Hilton can benefit from visiting at least two islands – Rangali and Rangalifinolhu – which are joined across the clearest blue lagoon by a 500-metre footbridge (the seriously lazy can just hop onto a dhoni, a boat that shuttles guests between the two). While both have incredible appeal, Rangali is the one with the The Over Water Spa. Not just any spa, mind you, but, in a country where opening newer, better, more exotic, more beautiful spas has almost turned into a competitive sport, Rangali is the most extraordinary of the lot.

A stunning setting almost in the middle of the ocean also has treatment rooms with glass floors through which you can watch the life of the ocean while enjoying a massage.

There are a few details that keep the spa at Rangali a few steps ahead of the competition. Firstly, it's managed by Chiva-Som, the renowned Thai health resort, the first of its kind in Asia. Secondly, three of its four treatment rooms have glass floors, so, instead of looking down onto a bowl of pebbles or lotus petals while you're having a massage or wrap, you can peer straight into the ocean and be distracted by all the wonderful marine life. For decades now, therapists, doctors, dentists and other healers have understood the relaxing effects of an aquarium (perhaps that's why so many waiting rooms have them). Consider then, how much better in the relaxation stakes it is to have nature's own aquarium (there are more than 700 species in these waters) to divert, amuse and calm while you enjoy a skin-softening treatment or a muscle-easing massage. The final thing that gives Rangali its edge is the sense of seclusion – there are just 50 water villas on the island, all built on stilts, all with their own private deck and stairs that lead you down into the lagoon. Should you feel so proprietorial that you begin to feel you never want to leave your villa, dinner or a barbecue will materialise, as if by magic, on your private terrace.

The spa itself offers a tantalising menu of exotic treatments that combine the best of Asian and European know-how. As might be

The spa is set way back from the resort
accessed by a long walkway to an
open-air Jacuzzi and a relaxation area

expected from a spa overlooking the ocean, a number of seawater and seaweed treatments are available. These include the phytomer seaweed re-mineralising body mask – a great exfoliater and a proven aid to cell renewal. It's especially good for sensitive skins as it contains a particularly gentle seaweed extract, tolerated by even those who may have previously been allergic to seaweed and iodine. Or try the exotically named Detoxifying Sea of Senses special, a detox treatment begins with a skin brushing, followed by the application of a warm algae mask all over the body. This procedure acts as a heat trap, which helps to eliminate excess fluids and toxins as well as softening the skin. As the mask performs its task, further relaxation comes your way in the guise of a scalp massage. At the other end of the body, I have to admit that anyone who does anything wonderful to my feet becomes my friend forever. So I heartily recommend the Oriental Foot Ritual. This fantastic treatment is a million miles away from any pedicure or foot massage you've ever had – it begins with a bathing and exfoliation of feet and legs, progresses through to a skin polish and finishes with a marvellous massage. When it's over, your feet and legs are cocooned in warm herb-infused towels – sigh.

It's difficult to make the most of the delights at the spa when the beach and reef beyond exert such a powerful lure, but, if you can only make time for just one treatment, make it the Pol-La-Mai Siam, a traditional Thai skin special. First, there's a gentle body scrub of Thai herbs and flowers, followed by a mask of exotic fruits: papaya, pineapple and aloe. The enzymes in the first two are great skin softeners and the aloe soothes and heals, especially if you've suffered any sun damage. While the mask continues to work, your hair and scalp are massaged with a remedial herbal mud. It's utter bliss and you won't want to move afterwards – take your time and, when you're ready, just shuffle back to your own private sundeck and daydream for a while. It's all part and parcel of the great joy of the Maldivian islands: each one is tiny enough for you to be able to see everything on the first day or two. After that, you can simply take it easy.

Spiritual

Ethereal

Pure

Refined

Unworldly

Perfect

So many people are enmeshed in a spiritual abyss and so many are trying to find a way out. They question their motives, values and way of life. They try to strip away the clutter in their lives, in their minds and in their souls as they look for a sense of peace and calm. To help them along the way they look at eastern philosophies and ancient wisdoms while they look for shamans, gurus and teachers. They head for the hills to meditate and bring a sense of perspective to their being and a sense of peace. They bathe in streams, pools and tumultuous seas as a type of cleansing and baptism.

More than anything they are searching for ways to calm the mind and cool the senses in a holistic fashion. Holistic therapies are an imperative part of any spa with a spiritual context and a good therapist while treating the body will also touch the mind.

In holistic terms the two can never be separate while the place which offers it must be calm, connected with its surroundings and guarantee peace and quiet. For while these visitors search for tranquillity of the mind, they also crave cosseting of the body – the spiritual spa excels at both.

Ananda, The Palace Estate, Narendra Nagar, Uttaranchal, India.

Ananda

F or centuries Rishikesh has been a place of pilgrimage. Set in a Himalayan valley close to the source of the Ganges, it is believed by many to be the birthplace of yoga, which is why so many ashrams have grown up around it. Each day the roads into town are packed with pilgrims laden with gifts of oils, rice and garlands of marigold and jasmine as they make their way to the temples. By their side are hundreds of sadhus, many of whom travel here from the other end of this vast sub-continent in order to offer up prayers in one of India's holiest places, and the odd westerner or two, travellers who have picked up the trail in their search for enlightenment.

High up on the slopes of the mountainside sits Ananda, over looking the holy Ganges. The word ananda comes from Sanskrit and means 'health and contentment', but here in the grounds of the Maharajah of Tehri Garwahl's summer palace, ananda has come to mean rest and rejuvenation. While the palace itself is a solid, stocky building of various influences, its setting is magical. The extensive grounds are dotted with meandering paths, soothing water features and places where you can pause to contemplate, meditate or simply wonder. An exquisite colonnaded pavilion provides the perfect setting for early morning yoga classes and is also used during the day for breathing and meditation exercises.

The spa itself is a modern structure surrounded by greenery and stands of bamboo that reach for the heavens. At the heart of its regime are a series of treatments based on ayurveda, the world's most ancient medical tradition. Here, under the direction of an ayurvedic doctor, treatments are prescribed once your body type has been established. People are considered to be a blend of the three doshas or elemental types: vata (air), pitta (fire) and kapha (water) – a balance of the three are believed to be integral to well-being, while any imbalance results in disease and distress.

Treatments are carried out in a series of rooms created specifically for their purpose. The ayurvedic area, for instance, features solid wooden massage tables, smooth as satin from many years of oil applications, while brass pots on wooden cradles hint at treatments like sirodhara and thakradhara. Both involve oil or buttermilk being dripped in an even stream onto the forehead to calm the mind and reduce stress. The oil-based sirodhara, a

If you have never experienced an ayurvedic treatment then this is the place to try one, whether it involves oils or herbs or indeed both, it will be unforgettable.

powerful treatment, is often mis-prescribed in Western spas that have little knowledge of what it can do to the nervous system – used inappropriately, it can leave you feeling twitchy and unable to sleep. The specialists at Ananda will not perform it on anyone on a very short stay, as they need to monitor your reaction to the treatments to determine whether or not you would benefit from it. I had the gentler thakradhara instead. It was not something I was looking forward to as the smell of the buttermilk is strong and acrid, yet within seconds I fell asleep – and stayed that way until gently awoken at the end of the treatment.

Other treatments include a synchronised massage known as abhyanga, in which two masseurs work in brisk tandem to rub a medicated oil all over your body, using firm, fast strokes – the oil itself contains herbs and spices that are blended to order according to your dosha. The pizhichil – another form of oil application – is gentler. One of the most relaxing massages known to man, this is carried out by a team of four masseurs and leaves you feeling sleepy, warm and thoroughly pampered.

Well-being is as much a state of mind as a matter of bodily health, and a great part of Ananda's philosophy is geared towards total relaxation and stress reduction, which is why yoga, pranayama (breathing) and meditation classes are such a vital part of a stay at the spa.

Those who've had enough pampering can take advantage of Ananda's location amid the splendour of the Himalayan foothills. There are special hiking trails for more active guests, or you can take it easy on one of the walks to the local temples – there is a glorious one at Kunjapuri, a mere hour or so away. But, whatever you do, don't miss a visit to the temples at Rishikesh for the arti, or evening prayers, a time when pilgrims from all over this vast sub-continent come to pray and make offerings as the sun sets behind the mountains and the tiny flames of their floating candles dot the Ganges like diamonds.

The
Source

Opulent fabrics, calm colours and tranquil shades highlight the care and attention lavished on the spa.

B egawan Giri is an extraordinary private estate just a few miles north of Ubud, the old capital and artistic heart of Bali. Of all the jewel-like Indonesian islands, Bali, with its sand-washed coastline and brilliant blue seas, is possibly the most beautiful. While it is this coastal beauty that initially attracts the majority of the island's visitors, what keeps them coming back is its exquisite interior of tiny villages, rushing rivers and still bathing pools, dense tropical jungle and rice terraces of such a vivid green that they seem to be carved from emeralds. The spiritual landscape is just as exhilarating. To the Balinese, spiritual awareness is as vital as breathing, so everywhere you go, you will find a wealth of shrines, altars and temples. Hardly a week goes by without some Hindu festival being celebrated – a banner will flutter in the distance, then a drum will sound and, gradually, a procession of celebrants, led by a priest, will make its way across a rice terrace, through a field and along the road to the local shrine.

Begawan has set out to capture the essence of Bali in teak and bamboo, coconut wood, ironwood, bronze and stone in a breath - taking setting that lies nestled among the trees that grow by the wild, rushing Ayung River. Legend has it that the forests in central Bali were too frightening and formidable for ordinary village folk and only three wise men – the begawantha – lived there, imbuing the place with a spiritual energy. Hence Begawan Giri's name – it means the 'Wiseman's Mountain'.

Designed by architect Cheong Yew Kuan, it took almost nine years to carve the first five residences out of the mountainside – tejasura, sound of fire; tirta ening, clear water; bayugita, windsong; wanakasa, forest in the mist; and umabona, house of earth in the wilderness. A further seven villas were added two years later. All are set within landscaped gardens, enclosed within their own walled gardens and enhanced with their own fountains and swimming pool, separate yet together. A main building, which houses a reception, restaurants and bar, sits proudly on an incline that overlooks the spring-fed pool of the water gardens. At the centre of the complex lies a huge open-air amphitheatre where local dancers, actors and musicians stage performances most evenings. The grounds are spectacular, merging seamlessly into the surrounding forests thanks to the transplantation of over 2,500 native trees, shrubs, ferns and flowers. Guests can explore the rainforest with a guided walk around the hiking trails that lead into its depths.

Far below the main grounds, bathed in the sounds of the Ayung, stands The Source, the estate's magical spa. Its treatment pavilions and traditional bales are open to the elements and echo with the sounds of birdsong and rushing water. Guests are surrounded by frangipani trees, orchids and hibiscus, and immersed in a ritual of massages, scrubs and treatments that make full use of native plant essences. Try a hibiscus and aloe vera treatment for hair and body; a Bali boreh spices ritual, which uses ginger, cloves and nutmeg; or enjoy the simple pleasures of a fresh papaya scrub or a honey and cucumber facial.

The treatment that keeps me coming back, though, is the taksu, a special Balinese deep-tissue massage whose strong, penetrating strokes really work the body. While it can be slightly uncomfortable if you're not used to it, take a few deep breaths and try to relax – you'll soon get used to the sensations. Taksu is particularly good for combating tight or tired muscles (especially useful if you've been cramped into a tiny plane seat for several hours), and leaves me feeling like I've just been given a shot of pure energy.

Each year a number of visiting masters arrive at Begawan to organise and teach specific classes and workshops – some in healing and meditation, others in yoga and psychic massage, pilates or self-healing. Yet others involve reiki training and avatar, in which participants are encouraged to seek awareness of their inner selves. Although some classes are relaxing and tranquil, others are rigorous and demanding – the latter are particularly favoured by those who come to Begawan in order to make adjustments to their lives and priorities.

In its setting, its architecture and its ethos, Begawan Giri Estate has managed to capture the gentle spiritual essence of Bali and create a haven of tranquil peace from which its guests return to the real world refreshed and reinvigorated in both body and soul.

The Lanna Spa , The Regent Chiang Mai, Thailand.

The Lanna Spa

T he most important city in northern Thailand, Chiang Mai blends the contemporary – high-rise office blocks and hotels, shopping malls and traffic jams – with everything a visitor might wish to find in one of the country's oldest cities: temples, craft workshops, more temples, ancient festivals and even more temples. It was within the walls of these temples that Thai massage was first practised and later refined.

In a world of its own, overlooking rice fields, mountains and temples, the Lanna Spa brings the best of Thai traditional know-how and therapies to the over-exhausted visitor.

One of the world's most ancient massage techniques, often called the yoga massage, Thai is based on the application of pressure along the energy lines of the body, together with a stretching of the muscles, which the therapist does using his or her body – the combination stimulates energy flow and eases tension. If I could only have one type of massage for the rest of my life it would have to be Thai, as it stretches those crumpled muscles and gets the blood racing round my body – I can literally feel the blocked channels opening up. I have to admit that there are times when I wonder if my body will ever recover from such rigours and contortions; but towards the end of the session, when I'm spread-eagled over the back of the therapist, I can practically feel the energy rushing through my body. Thai is one of the few massages in which the massagee stays fully clothed – a loose cotton pyjama suit is de rigueur – so that the therapist can get a good grip when applying pressure.

The place to enjoy Thai massage at its best is the bougainvillaea-draped Lanna Spa, which looks out across the rice fields and temple of Chiang Mai's Regent Hotel. Its seven spacious suites, each with its own herbal steam room, outdoor shower and tub, as well as a tropical rain-shower massage table, are where treatments are offered to couples and solo travellers alike. Designed in typical northern Thai style, all soaring roofs and painted doors, the suites are built of wood, mostly teak. The interiors are decorated with rich, dark silks highlighted with delicately placed fragments of gold leaf. And if the interiors are sumptuous, the exteriors are extraordinary. Just looking out across the rice fields from my massage table is enough to induce a trance-like state in me – especially if the hotel's family of water buffalo are ambling around in the background. This extraordinary quartet of Mrs Mud, her albino husband, Mr Sand, and their two offspring, Clay and Tui, have the run of the property and like

to proceed through the grounds once or twice a day, as if they were an Italian family out for a brief passeggiata.

Traditional herbs and aromatic oils are used in the spa's steam therapies, massages and rituals. In the steam room, for instance, a sage-like herb, bai nart, is used to clear headaches and soothe tensions; lemongrass is used to de-stress; morning glory helps clear sinuses and wild lime improves breathing. In massages, prai, a member of the ginger family with a sweet, woody fragrance, is used as a natural moisturiser; nutmeg, with its warming properties, helps ease aching muscles; while ylang-ylang is supposed to aid amorous endeavours, which is why it is often prescribed for couples. The spa also offers a glorious potpourri of body scrubs: there's the signature Lanna herbal body polish, in which a mix of sandalwood, prai, bai nart and lemongrass combine to leave your skin feeling like satin. For a more refreshing – and rather sensuous – experience, opt instead for the honey seed rub, a blend of lime, honey and sesame seeds. The smell alone is worth the price of admission.

Local clay, already rich in cleansing minerals and infused with sandalwood, is used in facials; as are aloe and lavender, the latter for its cooling properties and the former for its healing ones. These two ingredients are also used together in a body wrap that works wonders on both over-exposed skin and the undernourished variety. Once the mixture has been applied, the body is covered with banana leaves to help cool the skin and repair any cellular damage. The spa also has two great scalp treatments that make use of traditional ingredients. Wild lime hair care, which is based on the juices of freshly crushed lime, is an intensive reconditioner for dry, damaged or bleached hair, and also includes a head neck and shoulder massage, while the prai oil treatment is particularly good for dry, flaky scalps.

The spa also has a number of what it calls herbal aromatic retreats – each of which features at least two hours of serious pampering. But I have no problems choosing among the plethora of Lanna's treatments. Like I said earlier, I really can't go past the straight Thai massage for its unique ability to knock the kinks out my work-stressed body and set me on the road to true relaxation.

Sensuous

Lush

Voluptuous

Sybaritic

Sumptuous

Hedonistic

Pampering the senses is an important part of any spa. It must recognise that guests are there for a respite from the rigours of everyday living, that they are not just looking for comfort and care, they want it with silks and fragrance with beautiful sounds and gorgeous settings. They need unguents scented with musk and jasmine, warm herbal wraps in linens and muslins, the velvet of petals floating in warm baths.

They need the power of touch, one of the great natural healers. A truly gifted therapist knows at a touch what a body needs – what strength is required and what areas need work. The sensory journey practised within many spas, tells the therapist exactly what each body needs, as a series of fragrances are presented and discarded until the vital ones remain.

That guest needs to feel the heat of stones, which have been lying in deserts for millennia, and the silkiness of oil crushed from fruits and scented with flowers. That same body desires the warmth of the sun as it bathes in the open air as well as the coldness of ice in the shock of plunge pools. They need extremes of experience in voluptuous environs on balmy days in places redolent with sybaritic delights.

Thermae del Parco

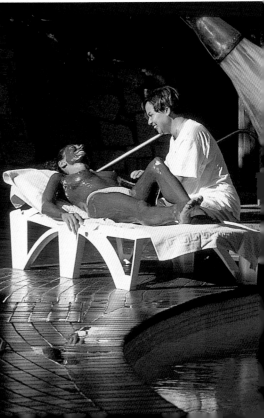

The second largest island in the Mediterranean, Sardinia has a wild heart. It's a landscape of mountains and macchiai, a wild grassland of dwarf oak, prickly pear and wild thyme that softens as you approach the white-sand shores of the coast. It is also an island of mystery – wherever you go you'll come across nuraghe, cone-like structures, reminders of a people who lived there almost 3,000 years ago and about whom almost nothing is known. If you head for the northwestern Costa Smeralda, however, you'll come across a far better-known tribe – the rich and famous, who flock here every August in their yachts. Turn in a southwards direction instead, and you'll end up in a place devoted to fun, health and well-being – the Forte Village Resort.

This luxurious playground has a choice of four five-star hotels, the same number of four-star hotels and an array of villas and cottages. There's plenty of restaurants and a vast selection of sporting activities available. As well as the standard swimming pools and tennis courts, there are water sports such as sailing, scuba diving, canoeing and windsurfing, while land-based attractions include an on-site go-kart track and a riding stable. The resort even has its own wildlife area, teeming with Patagonian penguins, peacocks, flamingos and parrots. But, best of all, it has what may well be the most exciting spa in Europe.

The Thermae del Parco is set in its own gardens, tropical with a dash of Zen, at the centre of which lie five seawater pools. Like the Dead Sea of Israel, the saline density of the water is so high that bodies float naturally. Once you've got used to the sensation, it creates a feeling of intense relaxation. Magnesium salts, a refined, patented sea oil and marine extracts all add their own therapeutic properties to the mix. Each pool is maintained at a constant, but different, temperature, ranging from 38°C to 20°C. Guests start off with a soak in the warmest pool and work their way gradually down the temperature gradient towards the energising cool pool. To assist the general sensuality of the experience, some pools have fountains that act as massage aids while others are plainer, focusing attention on the soothing sounds of the water as it runs over stones and splashes gently to the rhythm of the bodies within. Over the years physiotherapists have made use of the pools to heal some of the

most famous broken bones, torn ligaments and frayed muscles in European sports. A dry sand bath is often prescribed for its exfoliant properties as the perfect way to finish the five-pool float – it's warming, comforting and ultra-relaxing.

Forte Village is one of the leading Thalasso centres worldwide. With Thalassotherapy, a healing exchange takes place between the human body and the powers of the sea through the warmth of sea water. Vital essential minerals and trace elements supply us with new energy – they revitalise, heal and relax. At Thermae del Parco, the powers of the sea are applied to specially developed therapies which are devised to work in harmony with the healing properties of the pools. There is a whole menu of underwater massages enhanced with essential oils, seaweed or mud, yet others are combined with sea salt scrubs or special firming treatments. An extraordinary underwater shiatsu massage has been specially devised for the warmest pool – the therapist manipulates, stretches and works your body, while the water takes all the weight. It feels as if you're performing in some weird underwater ballet.

While the masseurs at most spas are brilliantly trained and have great technique, few are really gifted – and Guido, who works at the Thermae, is one of them. It takes him just a few seconds of gentle touch to find the seat of your stresses and tensions, and only a few minutes longer to start to ease them away. You might think the source of your problem lies in your lower back, for instance, but Guido knows better, heading straight for your calves instead – and minutes later, his magic has begun to do its work. Best of all, he doesn't hold with any of that new age whale music you normally get in spas – for him it's Puccini or nothing. Sadly, Guido's powers are no longer a well-kept secret, so book a session with him at the same time as you reserve your room.

While you're there, make sure you also remember to reserve some time to explore the island properly as the mountains are magnificent and the coastline breathtaking.

Something for every style and taste in this extraordinary resort of eight hotels as well as apartments and villas.

Jimbaran Bay

Beautiful unspoilt beaches, glorious forests and acres of rice terraces, which along with the gentleness of the people invite visitors to return again and again.

The sheer natural beauty of Bali, with its becalmed tropical beaches, dense rainforest and rivers that wash through the landscape in vast silvery ribbons, is enhanced by its aura of total serenity. This sense of spiritual peace comes mainly from the Balinese – their sweet-natured approach to life has exerted a pull on artists and poets down the ages, as well as on those who come to these islands seeking nothing more than a week in the sunshine.

Anyone in search of romance as well as relaxation would do well to head straight for the Four Seasons Resort at Jimbaran Bay – as far as I'm concerned, its villas are the most romantic in the world. This enchanting aura is conjured up, in part, by a sense of seclusion and spirituality, in tandem with an attention to detail that delights at every turn. A small shrine stands by the carved, painted door of each villa, and every morning the staff leave flowers and offerings for the Hindu gods who watch over this place. Behind lies a small garden, a plunge pool with an elephant-shaped fountain and a sun deck with views over the bay, as well as three pavilions. The first is an outdoor one for relaxing, dining, reading and relaxing; the second is an indoor one for dressing and sleeping, while a third provides both indoor and outdoor showers and baths.

The spa looks towards the ancient cultures of Indonesia for its inspiration. Ingredients for its massages and therapies include flowers, herbs and spices, all indigenous to the country's forests, mountains and islands. These essences and extracts, although blended from time-honoured recipes, are adapted for modern beauty treatments. All, that is, except for the jamu, which are potions made from various herbs and spices, offered at the end of each treatment. The men's version – the jamu pria – includes, among other ingredients, ginger, turmeric and chilli and is said to make the man stronger in every way. The women's jamu wanita also contains turmeric and ginger, seasoned this time with sour-sweet tamarind. Jamu wanita is believed to increase vitality as well as enhancing sexual prowess. You may choose to forego a taste of these exotic drinks, and swap them for some herbal tisanes or spicy tonics – but I reckon you should be a bit bold and try one. After all, you have come all the way to Bali for a taste of the exotic.

Many of the spa's treatments use essential oils based on flowers and spices grown in the resort's own gardens. All the ingredients sound good enough to eat. Take the coconilla skin scrub, for instance. This exfoliates and remoisturises dry, sun-soaked skin with a blend of freshly shredded young coconut, vanilla beans and coconut milk, all mixed together just before being applied to the body. Another scrub blends nutmeg with lemongrass and mint – quite delicious. Massages include the orient, a Balinese take on a Thai massage, in which no oil is used and where firm pressure is applied to all the energy meridians. The aroma massages offer a choice of two glorious essential oil blends – the peace of Bali is a mixture of sandalwood, ylang-ylang and spices, the Bali sunset is a blend of lavender, lemongrass and nutmeg. The signature Balinese massage is an absolute delight: the oil is scented with coconut, basil, vetiver and patchouli. Be prepared for pressure, though, as the traditional Indonesian massage style is firm, involving a mixture of long, kneading strokes, pummelling and skin rolling.

Although the royal lulur is now available all over the world, this is the place to have it. It was originally devised as a pre-wedding treatment for Indonesia's royal princess and was performed every day for 10 days before the wedding. At the Four Seasons, the lulur Jimbaran lasts for two hours and is an experience you will never forget. It begins with an intense Balinese massage, and is followed by an exfoliation with a scrub made from rice powder, ginger root, sandalwood and spices. When the mixture is finally rubbed off, you'll smell like the dish of the day, a point reinforced when you are splashed all over with yoghurt. Luckily, before you're trussed for the oven, the yoghurt is showered off and you are led to a warm, scented bath brimming with rose petals. As you soak in contented, aromatic silence, the therapist returns to wash you. I must admit, nobody had bathed me so conscientiously since my mother stopped doing it many years ago. It feels strange at first, but you soon learn to lie back, relax and enjoy. One final thing to remember – the Four Season's own special blend of treatments, design and seclusion combine to make this one of the most romantic hotels I've ever stayed in, so make sure that when you get there, the man of your dreams is right by your side.

Ancient Javanese bathing rituals, once the preserve of the royal family, are now available to all, while traditional Indonesian massage is not for the faint-hearted.

Two Bunch Palms Resort and Spa. California, USA.

Two Bunch
Palms

A sybarite's delight in Southern California so beloved of movie stars and ubermodels, but it is where the rest of us can come to be cosseted and pampered.

The deserts of southern California are, for the most part, inhospitable wastelands, save for the occasional oasis. Resorts such as Palm Springs sprung into being around these natural phenomena, their growth feeding on the constant supply of life-giving water. Two Bunch Palms, an oasis named after its twin clusters of palms by a team of army surveyors in the early years of the last century, is second to none as a centre of North American healing lore (with just a touch of the Wild West). It's the stuff of legend – a natural desert oasis deep in California's Coachella Valley, it brought respite and hope to the pioneers whose wagon trains pushed through to the Pacific Coast. Next came Al Capone and his gangsters, who reputedly built the bungalows that became the nucleus of the current resort; then, more recently, the place made a cameo appearance in director Robert Altman's great take on Hollywood, *The Player.*

The resort is built around a series of extraordinary natural hot springs, which come gushing out of the ground at 59ºC. The mineral-rich water is piped into the property through a series of artesian wells, then cooled to a range of temperatures in large tanks before it is allowed to flow into the pools, lakes and tubs that punctuate the grounds. The centrepiece is the GROTTO, which is deemed so important that it is always written in capital letters, where two adjoining areas of hot mineral waters are maintained at slightly different temperatures. The idea is that you move from the soaking pool, heated to a mere 34ºC, to the hot pool, kept at a constant 38ºC, to soothe your tired limbs, tense muscles and aching joints. Many also claim that the mineral-enriched water has a therapeutic effect on dull, tired-looking skin.

The southern Californian weather is, of course, the other great healer. Hot, dry desert air warms the resort's open-air pavilions and gazebos, as well as its pools and baths. You can choose to take your treatments here, shaded from the desert sun by the vast over-hanging branches of the tamarisk trees. Poolside cabanas and huge sunbins (the spa's own term for steep-sided enclosures where you can sunbathe in privacy) in the grounds provide ample opportunity for acquiring an all-over tan. Privacy and solitude are paramount at Two Bunch, so much so that there are strategically placed notices requesting guests to speak quietly. Those who fail to oblige are asked to leave, pronto, while mobile phones can only be used in the privacy of guests' bedrooms or cars.

Two Bunch also takes its location and reputation seriously. Its casitas, suites and villas are all built from natural materials, and decorated in what the management terms retro-bohemian style, a sort of simplicity that the mega-rich find endearing. While treatments are largely inspired by traditional holistic therapies from all around the world, many of them have been given a Californian twist. While many places, for instance, might offer you a choice of Swedish or shiatsu massage, only Two Bunch can give you the best-of-both-worlds option of a Swedish/shiatsu combo, a blend of the most beneficial aspects of both. While some spas occasionally seem to blend two different styles of therapy together for the sheer novelty value, this combination is firmly rooted in the therapeutic efficiencies of both – the long, deep strokes of Swedish massage work in tandem with the acupressure of the shiatsu to awaken your circulation and revitalise your limbs.

In total Two Bunch offers more than 45 treatments to choose from, including reiki, Thai massage, paraffin treatments for hands and feet, hot stone therapy, herbal steams and a clay masque, which uses a natural cleansing green clay that's exclusive to the spa. Two Bunch has also devised a number of water therapies that make full use of the hot springs, and its speciality is watsu, a water shiatsu. As we all know, shiatsu is one of the great massages ever, but although the original has stood the test of time, this newly devised water shiatsu is also fantastically good. The water takes your weight allowing the therapist to stretch and realign your body to greater effect. A watsu session in one of Two Bunch's mineralised pools it is positively miraculous – I promise you that by the end, you'll feel not only longer and leaner but also thoroughly invigorated. Should you acquire a taste for watsu, you will probably also appreciate the wassertanzen, an expanded form of watsu that involves the massagee remaining under water for short periods of time, and aqua soma, an underwater reflexology treatment that uses music to maximise its benefits.

Two Bunch's location makes this the ultimate celebrity hangout. But you don't have to be rich and famous to make the most of the place – just in need of warmth, privacy and a little bit of pampering.

Hélène
Spa

W ith all their accumulation of legend, myth and history, the islands of the Pacific are just made for romance. There are towering mountains, star-filled skies, swaying palms and translucent blue seas to delight the eye, the sounds are those of the winds and waves, while the scents are those of tropical jasmine and passionflower – it almost seems as if each island exists solely to fulfil the senses. You only need add to the equation the wisdom of the island cultures – centuries of knowledge of the healing properties of the natural resources, from volcanic clays to the essential oils of plants, flowers and fruits – to realise that these isles might have been created on purpose to heal both soul and body.

Native culture notwithstanding, it took a woman with the sophistication of Paris and a knowledge of European therapies at her fingertips to realise her vision to create the sexiest spa in the world. Hélène Sillinger took her years of experience in France and melded them with the sensuality of the South Seas to create the Hélène Spa on the island of Moorea in French Polynesia. Half-concealed in the lush planting of a landscaped tropical garden stands a group of fares, which were built in a formation aimed at maximising the natural energy-giving properties of sun, mountain and lagoon by means of a Polynesian version of feng shui.

Each fare is completely surrounded by vegetation – gentle breezes waft through clumps of plants, shrubs and flowers that provide just the right amount of privacy while still allowing the sun's rays and the beams of the moon to shine through. A sense of seclusion is also fostered at each treatment area by winding paths, vast boulders and plentiful bamboo screens over which passionflower vines, plumerias and jasmine tumble in a riot of scented colour. One open shower is so overhung with plants that entering it gives one the impression of walking into a painted tree, while the river bath built out of natural stones and rocks would not have looked out of place in the Garden of Eden – the craggy structure is raw and rugged, but its concealing curtain of foliage and flowers makes it a sensualist's delight.

Along with an international choice of treatments and therapies, there are a number of packages known as Polynesian escapes – these offer combined therapies for individuals or couples that last

Traditional fares (local style huts) where treatments take place are almost hidden among the lush tropical vegetation of Moorea.

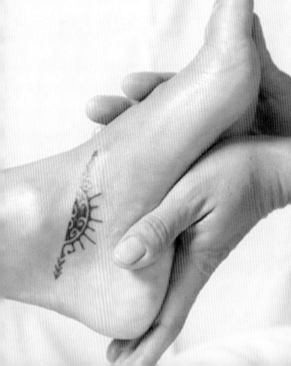

between one and four hours. These include mahana (sun), which prepares the skin for the rigours of a hard week's sunbathing with both the pulp and milk of fresh coconuts, among other exotic ingredients, all working together to get rid of dead skin cells and create a base for an even tan.

The here nui, or love escape, involves a purifying river bath à deux, as well as a massage using fresh coconut milk, and is especially recommended for lovers who've set their hearts on a traditional Polynesian wedding ceremony. Indeed couples come from all over the world for this most romantic of ceremonies, which takes place at sunset on a beach decorated with flowers and torches. The soon-to-be-weds are brought to the beach by canoe, where the groom's arrival is announced by the sound of a conch shell and the bride is accompanied by a group of women dancers dressed in grass skirts and garlands of flowers.

Nature's bounty plays a huge part in the treatments at Hélène Spa, for most of them use natural, locally produced ingredients, such as coconut fibre for cleansing and massage, river stones for massage, exfoliating sand from the lagoon and pineapple and papaya for scrubs and wraps, while lime fruits and flowers are used for purifying and hibiscus for hair care.

Spas exist to soothe the mind as well as the body, which is why I prefer to enjoy my treatments in one of the garden fares, surrounded by stunning views of the mountains, lush foliage and luxuriant flowers, brought to life with the tantalising hint of a breeze through the leaves and the distant thrill of birdsong. The only way to improve the experience is to go for a maeva Polynesian escape, which begins with a gentle papaya scrub to get rid of any dead skin cells. After the scrub has been showered off, you're smothered in a mix of more papaya and honey before being wrapped in banana leaves. While this might sound like a recipe for some kind of strange fruit salad, the enzymes in the banana leaves help your skin absorb all the goodness from the papaya and honey. A massage follows and the experience is completed with a warm flower-strewn bath for a truly heavenly experience.

Perhaps those tales of earthly paradise are true after all, and I've found it here in the Pacific.

Glossary

Acupressure massage

A Chinese massage which manipulates the body's pressure points to release blocked energies and to stimulate the flow of energy through the body.

Acupuncture

Part of traditional Chinese medicine, it employs the body's own energy to help heal itself. Using the same points as in acupressure tiny, fine needles are used to increase the flow of energy in the body.

Aerobic exercise

Any fat-burning exercise (such as brisk walking, running, cycling, spinning or dance) that uses the large muscle groups of the body and increases the heart rate to 50-90 per cent of its maximum.

Alexander technique

A method of re-aligning the body to improve posture, relieve tension and re-align the internal organs.

Aqua aerobics

Aerobic exercises performed in a pool using the support and resistance of the water to burn fat, strengthen bones, and increase cardiovascular activity. The buoyancy of the water reduces the chance of injuring joints or muscles.

Aromatherapy

Treatments such as massage, facials, body wraps or hydrobaths that include the application of fragrant essential oils. Different oils are used for different therapeutic benefits.

Asanas

Various yoga postures.

Ayurveda

One of the oldest medical disciplines in the world. Founded in India and now stretching worldwide, it incorporates a variety of techniques from meditation to massage and from diet to herbal medicines.

Balneotherapy

The use of underwater massage to stimulate, massage and relieve tension in the body.

Botox

A protein that is injected into the muscles of the face which freezes the muscles and helps minimise the appearance of lines and wrinkles.

Cathiodermie

Low-voltage electrical stimulation of facial area used to oxygenate the skin, stimulate and revitalise the circulation.

Collagen therapy

Injection of collagen beneath the skin with a fine needle to fill out wrinkles and lines.

Colonic

An intense water irrigation of the entire colon, intended to cleanse trapped impurities, preventing the recycling of toxins into the bloodstream.

Cranio-sacral therapy

A treatment that focuses on the connection between the skull and the base of the spine along the spinal column. It helps release trapped spinal fluid.

Crystal healing

The use of crystals to draw out imbalanced energy from the body.

Dead Sea Mud Treatment

An application of mineral-rich mud from the Dead Sea. Used to detoxify skin and body, and to ease painful symptoms of rheumatism and arthritis.

Dry brush

A brushing of the skin with a natural-bristle brush to remove dead skin and impurities while stimulating circulation, part of the preparation for massage, wraps or body masks.

Electrotherapy

Treatments using the stimulating properties of a low-voltage electric current on face and body.

Exfoliation

A process by which the top layer of dead skin cells is sloughed off the face or body whether by dry-brushing, scrubs or other exfoliation techniques.

Fango

The Italian word for mud. Used in treatments as a heat pack, which help detoxify the body, smoothe the skin, stimulate circulation and soothe tired or aching muscles.

Fitness profile/assessment

A test to evaluate the aerobic capacity, flexibility, and strength of a body, as well as resting heart rate, resting blood pressure, and body composition.

Flotation tank

A tank filled with enough salt water so a person can float in it; lights are either dimmed or turned off. The combination of a darkened room and the floating process is an aid to relaxation and stress reduction. Dry flotation treatments take place in a large bath or tank filled with water which are covered with a heavy waterproof blanket on which the body rests before the blanket is lowered into the water.

Four-handed or synchronized massage

A massage by two therapists working in synchronized movements along the body.

Frigi-thalgo

A type of wrap in which a cold (frigid) gel-like substance based on sea minerals and algae (thalgo) is smoothed on the body before it is wrapped in a heat-retaining waterproof sheet. The heat generated helps the body absorb some of the beneficial trace minerals from the algae.

Gommage

A cleansing, rehydrating treatment using creams and lotions, which are applied in massage-type movements.

Hammam

A Turkish or middle-Eastern bathing area which uses steam, water and oils.

Herbal wrap

A body wrap using strips of cloth that are soaked in a heated herbal solution and wrapped around the body. Part de-tox, part relaxation.

Holistic health

A philosophy of health that examines the physical, mental, emotional, and spiritual aspects of life and seeks to create a balanced approach.

Homeopathy

A form of medicine based on the principle that 'like cures like'. Patients are treated in minute quantities with natural substances that cause symptoms much like those manifested by the disease.

Hot spring

A natural, sometimes volcanic, spring of hot mineral water which has therapeutic properties and helps deal with sore or aching muscles.

Hydrotherapy

Treatments using water either in underwater massage, jet blitzes, showers and mineral baths.

Indian head massage

An ayurvedic therapy in which medicated oils are used in a vigorous head and scalp massage. It increases circulation, exfoliates the scalp and nourishes the hair. In its more western form it is less vigorous.

Ionisation

A thalassotherapy treatment in which seawater has been ionised with negative ions and is sprayed and/or inhaled; aids the upper respiratory tract.

Javanese Lulur

Sometimes called Balinese Lulur, it is a treatment originally devised for brides of the Javanese royal houses and took place each day for 14 days before the wedding ceremony. A mixture of massage, herbal exfoliation, yogurt splashes and a floral scented bath. Its aim is to relax, cleanse and nourish.

Jet blitz

A thalassotherapy treatment in which pressurised sea water is administered via a controlled hose in which each area of the body is massaged in turn to help boost circulation and break down fatty tissue.

Kneipp baths

Thermal treatments created by Father Sebastian Kneipp which use a mixture of hot and cold water as well as a number of herbal essences mostly to help increase circulation.

LaStone or hot stone therapy

A relaxing treatment designed to relieve stiffness and soreness and restore energy. Smooth, volcanic stones are heated and then used with oil in massage. Has its roots in Native American culture.

Lomi-lomi

A Polynesian healing treatment incorporating long and broad massage strokes, as well as a rocking motion, can be quite vigorous as the therapist uses forearms and elbows as well as hands.

Loofah scrub

A full-body scrub with a loofah, used to exfoliate the skin and stimulate circulation.

Lymph or lymphatic drainage

A special type of massage where a gentle pumping technique is used to help drain away pockets of water retention and blocked toxins.

Meditation

A form of mental discipline which can be practised in many different forms by concentrating on breathing, using a mantra etc. It helps reduce stress and tiredness and is beneficial to overall health.

Moor mud baths

A natural preparation that is rich in organic matter, proteins, vitamins and trace minerals, used to help ease aches and pains.

Oxygen facial

A facial that includes an application of a mist of liquid oxygen or capsules of oxygen-rich oils on mature, dry or sun-sore skins.

Paraffin treatment

A treatment in which heated paraffin wax is brushed over the body, feet or hands. It is used as a heat pack to help eliminate toxins as well as softening the skin.

Pilates

Devised by Dr Joseph Pilates to help damaged dancers, it is a series of precise movements performed on a specially designed apparatus to help strengthen and re-align the body as well as aiding flexibility. Exercises can also be done on a floor mat but are not as effective.

Qi Jong

A Chinese medical discipline which combines movement and breathing exercises which help strengthen both body and mind.

Reflexology

An ancient Chinese technique that uses pressure-point massage (usually on the feet, but also on the hands and ears) to restore the flow of energy throughout the entire body.

Reiki

A gentle Japanese technique of laying on of hands to help the energy flow within the body. Gentle and restorative.

Salt glow

A technique in which the body is rubbed with coarse salt, sometimes in combination with oil, as an exfoliant and to stimulate circulation.

Sauna

Dry heat administered in a wooden room to open the pores, relax muscles and eliminate toxins.

Seaweed wrap

A wrap or mask of concentrated seawater and seaweed, which helps release toxins and revitalise the skin.

Shiatsu

An acupressure massage technique developed in Japan. The therapist applies pressure to specific points in the body to stimulate and unblock 'meridians' or energy channels.

Swedish massage

The classic massage technique of manipulating muscles with the use of massage oils. It helps ease aching muscles, improve circulation and help relaxation.

Swiss shower

A treatment that involves powerful fine shower jets directed at the body from various heights, creating the effect of an invigorating massage.

Taksu

Massage indigenous to Bali. A strong, deep tissue treatment good for relief of tight or tired muscles.

Tai Chi

A Chinese martial art of stylised gestures regulated by deep breathing and movement.

Thai massage

One of the few massages where oil is not used, instead it is performed over light cotton pyjamas. A manipulation of the body using yoga-like stretching, pummelling and kneading as well as exerting pressure along the body's energy channels to help release blockages and soothe tight limbs and muscles.

Thalassotherapy

From the Greek for sea – thalassa, and treatment – therapia, all the treatments use seawater and seawater products such as seaweed and algae. True thallasotherapy centres have to be by the sea where the water, algae, mud et al are especially treated and purified for inclusion in the therapies. With this therapy, a healing exchange takes place between the human body and the powers of the sea through the warmth of sea water.

Tuina

A massage which is part of traditional Chinese medicine in which the body is pulled, pounded, pummelled and rolled. It works on the body's energy channels and helps release blocked energies. Vigorous and not for the timid.

Vichy shower

A light, rainlike shower, which is often used in combination with massage.

Watsu

A shiatsu massage treatment performed in a warm pool where the therapist holds and moves the limbs.

Wrap

A therapy in which the body is covered with lotions, oils, algae or mud then wrapped in a waterproof-heat inducing sheet, banana leaf or type of bacofoil, before being covered in blankets, (occasionally infra-red lamps are focused on the body) where the heat helps draw out toxins and impurities while at the same time the skin can absorb the minerals etc. from the mud or lotions. The effect is to remove toxins and soften the skin.

Yoga

An ancient Hindu discipline comprising focused deep breathing, stretching and toning the body using various positions designed to improve circulation, flexibility and strength. A philosophical approach to balancing the body and mind.

Directory

Elegant

The Better-Living Institute
Royal Parc Evian
South Bank of Lake Geneva
BP 8 – 74501 Evian-Les-Bains
Cedex, France
Tel: 00 33 4 50 26 85 00
Fax: 00 33 4 50 75 61 00
www.royalparcevian.com
reservation@royalparcevian.com

The Sanctuary
The Residence Mauritius
Coastal Road, Belle Mare, Mauritius
Tel: 00 230 401 88 88
Fax: 00 230 415 58 88
www.theresidence.com
reservation@theresidence.com

Il Centro Benessere
Grand Hotel Palazzo Della Fonte,
FiuggiVia Dei Villini,
7-03015 Fiuggi Fonte
(FR) Italy
0039 0775 5081
Fax: 0039 0775 506752
www.palazzodellafonte.com
information@palazzodellafonte.com

Clinique La Prairie
CH-1815, Clarens-Montreux,
Switzerland
Tel: 0041 21 989 33 11
Fax: 0041 21 989 33 33
www.laprairie.ch
info@laprairie.ch

Shambhala Spa
Parrot Cay
PO Box 164 Providenciales,
Turks & Caicos Islands,
British West Indies
Tel: 001 649 946 7788
Fax: 001 649 946 7789
parrot@tciway.tc
www.parrot-cay.com
www.comohotels.co.uk

Thalassa Spa
Anassa, Cyprus
P.O. Box 66006
CY-8830 Polis, Cyprus
Tel: 00 357 26 888 000
Fax: 00 357 26 322 900
www.thanoshotels.com
res.anassa@thanoshotels.com

Mandara Spa in Ocean Club
Ocean Club Resort
Ocean Drive, P.O. Box N4777,
Nassau, Bahamas
Tel: 001 242 363 2501 ext. 64808
Fax: 001 242 363 2424
www.mandaraspa.com
www.oceanclub.com
bahamas@mandaraspa.com

The SPA at Turnberry
The Westin Turnberry Resort
Ayrshire, Scotland KA26 9LT
Tel: 0044 1655 331 000
Fax: 0044 1655 331 706
www.turnberry.co.uk
turnberry@westin.com

Les Thermes Marins de Monte-Carlo
Société des Bains de Mer
(Hotel de Paris or Hotel Hermitage)
2, avenue de Monte-Carlo,
MC 98000 Principauté de Monaco
Tel: 00377 92 16 49 46
Fax: 00377 92 16 49 49
www.montecarloresort.com
thermes@sbm.mc

Exotic

The Spa at Las Ventanas al Paraíso
(part of Rosewood Hotels and Resorts)
KM 19.5 Carretera Transpeninsular,
San Jose del Cabo, Baja
California Sur 23400, Mexico
Tel: 0052 624 144 0300
Fax: 0052 624 144 0301
www.lasventanas.com
lasventanas@rosewoodhotels.com

The Spa, Amanjena
Route de Ouarzazate, km 12,
Marrakech, Morocco
Tel: 00 212 44 403 353 – direct to hotel
Amanresorts Global Reservations Office:
Tel: 0065 6887 3337
Fax: 0065 6887 3338
amanjena@amanresorts.com
www.amanjena.com
reservations@amanresorts.com

Mauna Lani Spa
Mauna Lani
68-1365 Pauoa Road, Kohala Coast, HI
96743
Tel: 001 808-881-7922
reservations@maunalani.com
www.maunalani.com
spa@maunalani.com

The Pavillion Spa, Lizard Island Resort,
Lizard Island, via Cairns, Queensland,
Australia
Tel: 0061 294186207
Fax: 0061299240944
www.poresorts.com

The Spa
Rajvilas – An Oberoi Resort Jaipur
Goner Road, Jaipur,
Rajasthan 303 012
India
Tel: 0091 141 680101
Fax: 0091 141 680 202
www.oberoihotels.com
reservations@rajvilas.com

The Serenity Spa
Las Dunas, Costa Del Sol
La Boladilla Baja, Carretera Cádiz
KM 163.500, 29689 Estepona,
Málaga, Espana
Tel: 0034 95 2794345
Fax: 0034 95 2794825
lasdunas@las-dunas.com
www.las-dunas.com

The Veyoge Spa
Kanuhura Resort & Spa
Lhaviyani Atoll, Republic of Maldives
Tel: 00960 230 044
Fax: 00960 230 033
www.kanuhura.com

Aroma Boma
Ulusaba Private Game Reserve
P.O. Box 71, Skukuza 1350 South Africa
Tel: 0027 13 735 5460
Fax: 0027 13 735 5171
www.ulusaba.com
safaris@ulusaba.com

Opulent

Assawan Spa
Burj Al Arab
P.O.Box 74147
Dubai, United Arab Emirates
Tel: 00 971 4 301 7777
Fax: 00 971 4 301 7000
www.jumeirahinternational.com
reservations@burj-al-arab.com

The Spa at Turnberry Isle
Turnberry Isle Resort & Club
19999 West Country Club Drive,
Aventura, Florida 33180-2401, USA
Tel: 001 305 932 6200
Fax: 001 305 933 6560
www.turnberryisle.com
reservations@turnberryisle.com

The Spa at Sandy Lane
Sandy Lane
St. James, Barbados,
West Indies
Tel: 001 246 444 2000
Fax: 001 246 444 2222
mail@sandylane.com
www.sandylane.com

Banyan Tree Phuket Spa
Banyan Tree Phuket
33 Moo 4 Srisoonthorn Road,
Cherngtalay, Amphur Talang,
Phuket 83110, Thailand
Tel: 00 66 76 324 374
Fax: 0066 76 324 375
phuket@banyantree.com
www.banyantree.com

Willow Stream
The Fairmont Scottsdale Princess
7575 East Princess Drive,
Scottsdale, Arizona, USA 85255
Tel: 001 480 585 4848
Fax: 001 480 585 0086
scottsdale@fairmont.com
www.fairmont.com

Serene

Polly Mar Beauty Spa
Kempinski Resort Hotel Estepona
Ctra. de Cádiz, km.
159, Playa el Padrón.
29680 Estepona (Málaga), Spain
Tel: 00 34 95 280 95 00
Fax: 00 34 95 280 95 50
info@kempinski-spain.com,
www.kempinski-spain.com

The Spa at Soneva Gili
Soneva Gili Resort & Spa
Lankanfushi, Northe Malé Atoll,
Republic of Maldives
Tel: 00 960 440 304
Fax: 00 960 440 305
sonresa@sonevagili.com.mv
www.six-senses.com/soneva-gili

Givenchy Spa
Le Saint Géran,
Poste de Flacq, Mauritius
Tel: 00230 4011688
Fax: 00230 4011668
www.saintgeran.com
infostg@sunresort.com

Chiva-Som
Chiva-Som International Health Resort
73/4 Petchkasem Road, Hua Hin,
Prachuab Khirikham 77110, Thailand
Tel: 0066 3253 6536
Fax: 0066 3251 1154
www.chivasom.com
reservation@chivasom.com

Canyon Ranch Spa and Health Resort
8600 E. Rockcliff Road, Tucson,
Arizona 85750, USA
Tel: 001 520 749 9000 (Worldwide)
Fax: 001 520 749 7755
www.canyonranch.com

Willow Stream
The Fairmont Banff Springs
P.O. Box 960 Banff Alberta,
Canada T1L 1J4
Tel: 001 403 762 2211
Fax: 001 403 762 4447
www.fairmont.com
banffsprings@fairmont.com

Aman Spa, Amanpuri
Pansea Beach,
Phuket, Thailand
Amanresorts Global Reservations Office:
Tel: 0065 6887 3337
Fax: 0065 6887 3338
Tel: 00 66 76 324 100/324 200
(direct to Amanpuri)
amanpuri@amanresorts.com
reservations@amanresorts.com
www.amanresorts.com
www.amanpuri.com

The Spa Village
Pangkor Laut Resort
Pangkor Laut Island,
32200 Lumut, Perak, Malaysia
Tel: 00605 699 1100
Fax: 00605 699 1200
www.pangkorlautresort.com

Aveda Concept Spa
Strawberry Hill Resort
New Castle Road, Irish Town, Jamaica
Tel: 001 876 944 8400
Fax: 001 876 944 8408
strawberryhill@islandoutpost.com
www.islandoutpost.com/StrawberryHill
reservations@islandoutpost.com

The Over Water Spa
Hilton Maldives Resort & Spa
Rangali Island, PO Box 2034,
South Ari Atoll, Republic of Maldives
Tel: 00 960 450629
Fax: 00 960 450 619
thespa@maldiveshilton.com.mv
www.maldives.hilton.com

Spiritual

Ananda – In The Himalayas
The Palace Estate, Narendra Nagar,
Tehri Garhwal, Uttaranchal, 249175, India
Tel: 0091 1378 27500
Fax: 0091 1378 27550
anandaspa@vsnl.com
www.anandaspa.com

The Source
Begawan Giri Estate
PO. Box 54, Ubud 80571
Bali, Indonesia
Tel: 0062 361 97 8888
Fax: 0062 361 97 8889
www.begawan.com
reservations@begawan.com
TheSource@begawan.com

The Lanna Spa
The Regent Chiang Mai Resort and Spa,
Thailand
Mai Rim-Samoeng Old Road Mai Rim,
Chiang Mai 50180, Thailand
Tel: 0066 53 298-181
Fax: 00 66 53 298-189
www.regenthotels.com
cm.reservations@fourseasons.com

Sensuous

Thermae Del Parco
Forte Village Resort
SS 195 km 39,600 – 09010 S.
Margherita di Pula (CA),
Sardinia, Italy
Tel: 0039 070 92171 / reservations desk:
0039 070 921 516
Fax: 0039 070 921246
Forte.Village@lemeridien.com
www.fortevillageresort.com

The Spa
Four Seasons Resort
Bali at Jimbaran Bay
Jimbaran 80361, Bali Indonesia
Tel: 00 62 361 701010
Fax: 0062 361 701020
www.fourseasons.com

The Spa
Two Bunch Palms
The Natural Hot Springs Resort & Spa
67-425 Two Bunch Palms Trail,
Desert Hot Springs,CA, 92249 USA
Tel: 001 760 329 8791
Fax: 001 760 329 1317
www.twobunchpalms.com
whiteowl@twobunchpalmscom
(for reservations)

Hélène Spa
Moorea Beachcomber Inter-Continental
Resort
BP 1019 – 98729 Moorea, French Polynesia
Tel: 00 689 55 19 70
Fax: 00 689 55 19 80
www.spa-tahiti.com helenespa@mail.pf

Second Edition
First Published 2003 by Dakini Books Ltd

211 - 212 Piccadilly
London W1J 9HG
T 020 7830 9692
F 020 7830 9693
www.dakinibooks.com

Publisher Lucky Dissanayake
Author Jo Foley

Advisor Dr. Peggy E. Furst-Mahne, Germany
Editor-in-Chief of SENSES - The international Wellness Guide Verlag, Stuttgart
Sub Editor Annie Mehra
Photo Editor Mani Suri and Margaret Buj
Proofing Tara Horan
Design Mani Suri and SMITH
Printed and Bound Europe

A CIP catalogue record for this book is available from the British Library

Library of Congress Cataloguing in Publication Data available.

ISBN 0-9537032-4-X

Picture Credits

Elegant
Evian-les-Bains, France
  J. N. Reichel, J. J. Liégeois, N. Bouchut
The Residence, Mauritius
  Photographs courtesy of The Residence
Palazzo della Fonte, Italy
  Mauro Galligani & Diego Banchetti
Clinique La Prairie, Switzerland
  Photographs courtesy of Clinique LPrairie
Parrot Cay, Turks & Caicos
  Martin Morrell & Francine Fleischer
Anassa, Cyprus
  Photographs courtesy of Anassa Resorts
Ocean Club, The Bahamas
  Photographs courtesy of Mandara Spa
The Westin Turnberry Resort, Scotland
  Photographs courtesy of The Westin
  Turnberry Resort
Les Thermes Marins de Monte Carlo
  Ralph Hutchings, Alain Dovifat, Bruno
  Fabbris, Jean-Jacques L'Heritier

Exotic
Las Ventanas al Paraiso, Mexico
  Photographs courtesy of Las Ventanas
Amanjena, Morocco
  Photographs courtesy of Amanresorts

Mauna Lani, Hawaii
  Thomas Barwick
Lizard Island, Australia
  George Apostolidis P&O Australia Resorts
Rajvilas, India.
  Photographs courtesy of Rajvilas
Las Dunas Beach Hotel & Spa, Spain
  Paul Dahan
Kanuhura Resort & Spa, Maldives
  Photographs courtesy of Kanuhura
  Resort & Spa
Ulusaba, South Africa
  Elizabeth Delliére

Opulent
Burj Al Arab, Dubai
  Photographs courtesy of Burj Al Arab
Turnberry Isle, Florida
  Photographs courtesy of Turnberry Isle
  Resort & Club
Sandy Lane, Barbados
  Photographs courtesy of Sandy Lane
Banyan Tree, Thailand
  Photographs courtesy of Banyan Tree
  Hotels & Resorts
The Fairmont Scottsdale Princess, USA
  Photographs courtesy of The Fairmont

Scottsdale Princess
Kempinski Resort Hotel Estepona
  Michael Reckling & Jane Munroe
Soneva Gili Resort & Spa, Maldives
  Ulli Schonart, Jean Marc Tinguad,
  Kiattipong Panchee, Vichit Yantapanit
Le Saint Géran, Mauritius
  J.B. Adoue, R. Jiles, D. Ham,
  D. Mendelsohn, R. Van Der Meeren,
  J. Nicholson, A. Osmond-Evans,
  C. Rodriguez, M .Shadow, R. Starr,
  P. Tosselli, M. Wilson

Serene
Chiva-Som, Thailand
  Photographs courtesy of Chiva-Som
  Luxury Health Resort
Canyon Ranch, Arizona
  Photographs courtesy of Canyon Ranch
The Fairmont Banff Springs, Canada
  Photographs courtesy of The Fairmont
  Banff Springs
Amanpuri, Thailand
  Photographs courtesy of Amanresorts
Pangkor Laut, Malaysia
  Photographs courtesy of YTL Hotels &
  Properties Sdn. Bhd.

Strawberry Hill, Jamaica
  Tim Street-Porter & Cookie Kinkead
Hilton Maldives Resort & Spa
  Glenn Aitken & Juergen Gutowski

Spiritual
Ananda, India
  Photographs courtesy of Ananda in the
  Himalayas
Begawan Giri, Bali
  Photographs courtesy of Begawan Giri
The Regent Hotel, Chiang Mai, Thailand
  Photographs courtesy of Regent Hotels
  Chiang Mai

Sensuous
Forte Village Resort, Sardinia
  Photographs courtesy of Forte
  Village Resort
Four Seasons Jimbaran Bay, Bali
  Photographs courtesy of Four Seasons
  Jimbaran Bay
Two Bunch Palms, California
  Photographs courtesy of Two Bunch
  Palms, California
Heléne Spa
  Photographs courtesy of Heléne Spa